A SURREY GARLAND

Customs, Traditions and Folk Songs from the Surrey of Yesteryear

MATTHEW ALEXANDER

COUNTRYSIDE BOOKS

NEWBURY BERKSHIRE

COUNTRYSIDE BOOKS
3 Catherine Road
Newbury, Berkshire

To view our complete range of books,
please visit us at
www.countrysidebooks.co.uk

ISBN 1 85306 853 5

To

Henriette-Marie

All photographs from Guildford Museum
unless otherwise credited

Produced through MRM Associates Ltd., Reading
Typeset by Jean Cussons Typesetting, Diss, Norfolk
Printed by Woolnough Bookbinding Ltd., Irthlingborough

Contents

Introduction   6

1   The Dark Days – Winter and Lent   13

2   Renewal – Spring and Easter   36

3   Holidays – May Day and Whitsuntide   55

4   Warmth and Light – Midsummer to Autumn   73

5   Harvests and Bonfires – The Fall of the Year   90

6   The Christmas Season   110

Index   127

Modern county boundary

Chertsey

Bagshot

Chobham

Camberley

Woking

Pyrford

Pirbright

Worplesdon

West Hors[l]

Merrow

Guildford

Puttenham

Albury

Gom[e]

Badshot Lea

Sher

Farnham

Compton

Farncombe

Wonersh

Elstead

Godalming

Bramley

Milford

Shamley Gree[n]

Frensham

Witley

Hascombe

Ewhurst

Thursley

Hambledon

Cranlei[gh]

Devil's Punch Bowl

Hindhead

Dunsfold

Alfold

Haslemere

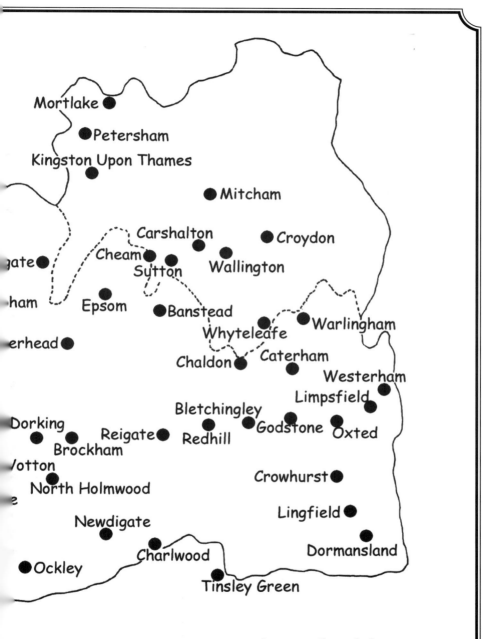

Mortlake

Petersham

Kingston Upon Thames

Mitcham

Carshalton   Croydon

Cheam
Sutton   Wallington
gate

ham   Epsom   Banstead   Warlingham

erhead   Whyteleafe

Chaldon   Caterham

Westerham

Limpsfield

Bletchingley

Dorking   Reigate   Redhill   Godstone   Oxted

Brockham

Wotton

North Holmwood

Crowhurst

Lingfield

Newdigate

Charlwood   Dormansland

Ockley

Tinsley Green

Map of Old Surrey

INTRODUCTION

If there were a single date, a single moment when old Surrey was replaced by the new, then it would be 4th August 1914. Hardly a Surrey village is without its war memorial, testifying to the numbers of men who never came back from the First World War – often depressingly large numbers in proportion to their small communities. Their absence prompted the increased mechanisation of farming and their womenfolk took on roles which were once the preserve of men. Farm girls who had been raking hay during the long golden summers of Edward's reign, dressed in their long cotton gowns and sun bonnets, were now wearing corduroy breeches and sitting astride the seat of a spluttering tractor.

By this time, education had already begun to effect social change. Illiteracy had played an important part in preserving a local culture. After all, if your information was obtained only from the people you met, then influences from afar were necessarily limited. In 1844 it was said that only one Surrey labourer in fifteen could read or write. Instead of signing their own names, they would mark official documents with a cross. The educational reforms of the 1870s and 1880s set out to change that, and with a high degree of success. By the end of Queen Victoria's reign, no village was without a school, and no child without a place in it. Those responsible for teaching had no doubt that the old culture was backward and belonged in the past, and that foolish superstitions ought to be replaced with educated common sense.

The coming of the railways had already transformed a poor, rural county into a wealthy residential area looking to London for its prosperity. At the same time, other factors led to a decline in agriculture. From being the major employer of labour, farming is now the occupation of only a tiny proportion of Surrey workers.

INTRODUCTION

Box Cottage at Caterham was no doubt attractive to passers-by, but probably an uncomfortable place in which to live.

By the outbreak of the Great War, many of the old customs had gone.

What, then, was Surrey like before these changes? Essentially, a farming county with poor soils. Much of the land was, and still is, infertile heaths and commons. The dry, sandy soil around Bagshot and the Greensands to the south of the Downs were useless for anything but rye and the tough 'heathcropper' sheep. Beef cattle could be raised on the clay soils of the Low Weald; while the poor uplands of the High Weald towards the Sussex border supported sheep. The chalk of the North Downs was crowned with light, dry loams that were suitable both for sheep and barley. The alluvial clays towards the Thames were more productive, with market gardens, dairy farms and hay meadows to supply London. Farms tended to be small, with perhaps 200 to 300 acres.

From the earlier 1870s, the economic depression that affected British farming generally was acutely felt in Surrey. Imported grain sent prices falling, and the manufactured products of the industrial cities eroded local crafts. Farm workers left the land as incomes fell – often not just the land, but the country as well. As they emigrated, their places (in other words, their picturesque cottages) were taken by newcomers whose income was earned far from the soil.

Old Surrey had few major aristocratic families with large estates. One result of this pattern of small-scale land ownership was that the improvements in farming methods, sometimes called

This red-brick building, with its Gothic windows, was typical of dozens built in the villages of Surrey in the second half of Victoria's reign.

the Agricultural Revolution, were slow in being adopted in our county. Despite the proximity of the great market of London, much of Surrey was isolated and even backward in its farming techniques. For example, the riots which swept Kent at the end of the 1820s were directed at smashing the threshing machines which threatened the farm workers' winter jobs. They had little impact in Surrey, because few farmers had invested in such new-fangled devices and continued to thresh by hand with the flail.

Many farm labourers relied on their rights on the common land to collect firewood and peat to warm their cottages, and perhaps to raise a few geese. The legally-enforced enclosure of these

A scene in Compton in the 1880s. The gentry stand proudly at their gate while the labourers watch from the background.

commons robbed the cottagers of these rights, justified by the claim that such Acts of Parliament were necessary 'to overcome the pattern of ancient ignorance'. Be that as it may, it was perhaps inevitable that it was only the profitable commons nearer London that were enclosed. Surrey today still has a large area of unenclosed common land.

Despite the lack of great aristocratic estates, there were numerous large houses, so that the wealthy classes of London might have country seats. The people of Surrey were thus largely either gentry or their tenants who worked their land. Outside the towns, there were few of the professional or commercial kind that occupied the middle ranks of society. It is curious to think that Surrey, now considered the classic middle-class county, had then almost no middle class at all.

The villages of old Surrey were small, intimate communities. Outside the urbanised north-east, even the market towns were of modest size. Guildford, the ancient county town, could not act as a true centre for Surrey. It lay, as it has always lain, in the economic shadow of London. As the Surrey towns were touched by the magic wand of the railway, however, they began to grow in size and expand in population as more and more incomers settled in them. People found they could live in a quiet country town and still travel to work each day in London – as what are now called 'commuters' but then were known as 'daily breaders'.

Although the towns grew rapidly, the villages remained small. They had to wait for the motor car to make them accessible to the influx of newcomers. As a result, it was not until the 1920s that village housing began to be developed significantly. Up until the First World War, some elements of local culture survived in village communities.

How far, then, are we able to reconstruct the ways and beliefs of the people of old Surrey? There are few alive today who had direct experience of them, and little systematic recording was done at the time by the early collectors of folklore. 'Folklore' is a term used to embrace the traditions, customs, superstitions and beliefs of (usually) the rural poor. Perhaps a better expression would be 'the culture of the people' because essentially that is what it is. Culture, whether of the urban rich or the rural poor, is a significant factor in everyone's life, a key element of social history and one worthy of exploration.

However, Surrey was largely ignored by the early folklorists. By 1900 the county had already gained an irredeemably middle-class reputation, a kind of suburban No Man's Land between the city culture of London and the real countryside beyond. 'Surrey may truly be said to be one of the least superstitious of the counties of England,' claimed one writer in that year. He was quite wrong, of course, but he typifies an attitude still met with today. English folklorists looked to the northern counties and the West Country for tales, superstitions, dialect and songs. Surrey was passed over in silence.

Charcoal burners in woodland near West Horsley in 1910. Their way of life and the demand for their product was already fading.

Rather than concentrating on the origins of a custom, it is more useful to understand the value of the custom to the people who observed it. The idea that some early folklorists put forward (that villagers did the same thing each year simply because they always had done so and had lost sight of the original reason) is nonsense. To give a few examples: taking part in these customs would show that the individual participants were part of a wider community, with its own identity. Social distinctions between the employer and his men, the squire and his farm workers, could be temporarily forgotten in sharing a drink. A door-to-door collection of money was made legitimate by being part of a recognised custom. These were immediate and present motives, without reference to some forgotten and misty antiquity.

This book describes some of the customs that were observed in some parts of Surrey at some point in the past. It must not be imagined that all were carried out everywhere and always. In fact, each area had its own local calendar, its own special days, based on the type of farming and its seasonal work, on church festivals and local fairs. Some customs are still celebrated today – Christmas above all. Others have disappeared with the passing of the rural society that produced them.

The reader should bear in mind that the boundaries of Surrey have been changed several times since the mid 19th century – most dramatically when the north–eastern parishes were removed when the London County Council was formed in 1889. For the purposes of this book, 'Surrey' is the county that existed from 1889 until 1965. It excludes the truly urban parishes, but recognises those that were submerged by the Greater London Council. Of course, folklore laughs at county boundaries. Almost everything found in Surrey can be found in neighbouring counties, and much can be found throughout England. Nevertheless, Surrey had its own distinct character, which I hope the following pages will show.

Matthew Alexander

CHAPTER 1

The Dark Days: Winter and Lent

The country year has its own times and seasons. It is never easy to decide when to begin an account of the turning year, where to cut into that everlasting circle of the seasons. The Church's year, for instance, begins with the first Sunday in Advent – around the beginning of December – which most would consider the end of the year. New Year's Day falls within the twelve days of Christmas, and is best considered with them. It could be argued that the agricultural year begins when the harvest has been brought in and the winter ploughing prepares the land for a new season.

Perhaps it would be simplest to consider the end of the Christmas holidays as marking the beginning of a new year, when the farm labourers returned to work after the feast of Epiphany. On arable farms, the horse teams would be led out with their ploughs. The fields would probably have been ploughed already, after the harvest, and the winter frosts would have broken up the hard clods. The January ploughing would prepare the fine tilth needed for sowing the next crop. The geology of Surrey is complex, and soil types vary from place to place quite dramatically. Each area tended to have its own design of plough to suit local conditions. On the heavy clay soils, oxen were often used in place of horses. While oxen are less intelligent than horses,

Ploughing at Badshot Lea around 1890. Hop poles
can be seen in the background. (Chrispics)

and need constant goading to keep them moving, they alone have
the massive strength to draw the plough-share smoothly through
the sticky clay.

The first date in the calendar that claims our attention is 20th
January, the eve of the feast of St Agnes. She was a young Roman
Christian who refused to marry, dedicating her life to Christ
instead. Because of this, she became the patron saint of young
girls and the eve of her feast day was a popular time for girls (and
perhaps occasionally young men) to foretell whom they might
marry.

Like many such superstitions, the ritual was considered more
effective if carried out while hungry. Fasting on St Agnes' Fast
was a common custom, and John Aubrey, who recorded many
miscellaneous observations in Surrey, gives this account of it in
1696: 'On St Agnes' night, take a row of pins, and pull out every

Dorking High Street in the early 1900s. Although only horse transport can be seen, the sign to the right shows that the motor car was already in evidence.

one, one after another, saying a Pater Noster, or sticking a pin in your sleeve, and you will dream of him, or her, you shall marry.' It is faintly curious, by the way, that Aubrey refers to a 'Pater Noster' a century and a half after the Lord's Prayer had replaced the Latin form. Perhaps the magical incantation of a mysterious language was felt to add some special power to the ritual.

Candlemas falls on 2nd February, when the medieval church celebrated the presentation of Christ in the temple, with a candlelight procession. The Reformation put out those candles, but the name survived. The day became associated with rhymes supposed to predict the weather – always a matter of the highest concern in a farming society. Fine weather on Candlemas Day was considered a bad omen. In Dorking the rhyme went:

If Candlemas Day be fair and bright,
Winter will have another flight.
If Candlemas Day be clouds and rain,
Winter will not return again.

Another version was grimmer still:

As far as the sun shines in on Candlemas Day,
So far will the snow blow in afore old May.

St Valentine's Day, on 14th February, is one of the old dates still celebrated today. The people of Surrey believed that was the day the birds chose their mates, and so was a fitting day to think of love and marriage. The superstition ran that the first person you saw that day would be your 'valentine' – often with amusing results. Of course, most preferred carefully to select someone as the object of their attention. Keeping your eyes firmly shut until the loved one was present was a obvious tactic, and some blindfolded themselves and were led to the house of the person they fancied in a very obvious display of intent. For those who could write – and this would have been less than half the population of the county until the 1870s – then a love letter became the custom from Georgian times. The practice of sending printed cards developed in the middle of the 19th century, encouraged by the cheaper 'penny post' .

As well as St Agnes' Eve, St Valentine's Day was a fitting time for girls to attempt to discover whom they were destined to marry. 'Husband-divining' rituals are perhaps the most varied of all superstitions (together, that is, with omens that foretell death). One was noted in Compton in the middle of Victoria's reign. It seems to have a flavour of witchcraft about it. A little before midnight the girl would prick a candle with pins, reciting:

The Dark Days: Winter and Lent

'Tis not the wax I mean to stick:
My true love's heart I seek to prick.
I wish him neither rest nor peace
Until he comes to me, and speaks.

The Surrey Magazine recorded in 1900 that: 'In bygone days another strange custom was practised on St Valentine's Eve, in order for a girl to discover her lover. She plucked five bay leaves, and when she went to her room for the night she pinned them on her pillow. One was stuck at each corner and one in the middle. This charm, it was said, caused the girl to dream of her future husband … Surrey maidens do not, as a rule, now adopt this and other simple methods which were believed in formerly, but they consult palmists and gypsies when they wish to satisfy their curiosity in such matters. There are, however, still a few in remote country villages who inherit a faith in some strange practices from their grandparents.'

Of course, a girl's heart can change. The first verse of a folk song collected in Elstead runs:

First I lov'd Thomas and then I lov'd John
And then I lov'd William, he's a clever young man;
With his white cotton stockings and low ankle shoes
And he wears a blue jacket wherever he goes.

Now the year turns to the traditions associated with Lent and Easter. Easter is, of course, a moveable feast and can fall on any day between 21st March and 25th April. This rather bewildering variation results from the fact that the death and resurrection of Christ took place at the Jewish feast of Passover. The date of this was determined each year by the phases of the moon, not by a fixed day in the calendar. The early Christians adopted the custom

St Mary's, Mortlake, from whose tower the Pancake Bell rang out.

of celebrating Easter on whatever day corresponded to the feast of Passover. In fact, the date was often difficult to calculate, and there were many disagreements in the Church about how exactly to arrive at it. Nevertheless, the date of Easter determined the major festivals of the spring: Shrovetide, Easter itself, and Whitsun.

Shrove Tuesday was the last opportunity for celebration and indulgence before the austere weeks of Lent. It takes its name from the medieval tradition of going to confession that day to be 'shriven', or absolved, by the priest. The Reformation saw the end of this custom, but in some places the church bell continued to be rung on Shrove Tuesday morning at the time that confession used to be heard. One such place was Mortlake, where until about

1950 the bell was rung for the half-hour before noon on Shrove Tuesday.

At Mortlake and elsewhere, it was known as the 'pancake bell', a reference to the custom of mixing the batter then for the evening pancakes. The original intention was to use up the remaining household stocks of sugar, butter, cream and other indulgent foods, and to build up the body before the Lenten fast began. In the 1860s George Sturt remembered his mother putting a little beer into the pancake batter at his childhood home in Farnham. For many Surrey people today, Shrove Tuesday remains 'Pancake Day', one of the few old traditions still widely observed. On the other hand, a new tradition has grown up fairly recently: that of pancake races. Competitors, often housewives, will race against

*Banstead was the only Surrey village where
children went 'shroving'.*

each other, carrying frying pans with pancakes. In theory, the pancake must be tossed continually but catching an airborne pancake while running is a very demanding skill indeed, and disasters are common. These races have a longer tradition in the Midlands, but even there they do not seem to go back much before the Victorian era.

One Shrove Tuesday custom recorded only in Banstead is 'shroving'. This involved local children going from door to door asking for money. As we shall see, this was a common element of many customs. The gooding collections were reserved for old people, usually widows, but shroving, like the May garland tradition, belonged to the young. It has been noted in Hampshire, Berkshire and Hertfordshire but in Surrey it appears to have been established only at Banstead. Elsewhere, verses similar to the May garland rhymes were chanted, but, if this was the case in Banstead, they have not been recorded. The headmaster of Banstead School noted in the logbook in 1871: 'Shrove Tuesday. Many of the boys and girls away. Shroving is an old custom in this village.' Old or not, it does not seem to have long survived the disapproval of the school authorities and the Victorian dislike of begging.

While we may regret the passing of many traditions, most of us will be glad that at least some are extinct. In particular, cruelty to animals was all too often considered an entertainment in the past. In defence of the people of old Surrey, it must be said that in a society where the regular slaughtering of family pigs, the wringing of hen's necks and the trapping of rabbits were simply stages in preparing a meal, sentimentality was rarer then than today. However, few would condone the old Shrove Tuesday sport of cock-shying or cock-threshing. This meant tethering a cockerel by a leg, and then pelting it from a distance with sticks or stones until it died. Whoever actually killed the bird was allowed to take it home to eat as part of the evening feast. In Alfold, the churchyard was the scene for this sport and on one occasion a wildly-thrown stone hit and killed, not the cock, but the son of the rector.

The churchyard of St Nicholas, Alfold, where the rector's son was killed while cock-shying on Shrove Tuesday.

The most characteristic, and the most spectacular, sport associated with Shrove Tuesday, however, was street football. It was played in many of the towns of northern Surrey in the early 19th century; most notably at Kingston-upon-Thames, where it attracted players and spectators from a wide area, including

*The narrow lanes of Kingston-on-Thames were a cramped
and dangerous playing field for mass football – until
a stop was put to it by the authorities.*

London. Shrove Tuesday football as played in Surrey had few
rules. Usually one half of the town played against the other half,
although there was no limit to the numbers on each side. The ball
was kicked off or thrown in at a central spot at a fixed time.

THE DARK DAYS: WINTER AND LENT

*Taffer Boult's band in 1895. They paraded the streets of Dorking
on the morning of Shrove Tuesday, collecting contributions
and displaying the three footballs on their frame.*

Rather than kicking the ball through your opponents' goal, the
intention was either to get it to your own goal (often a stream) or
to keep the ball in your own half of the town when the time to
finish came.

The players surged through the streets of the town, in a
disorderly and frequently violent mob. With dozens of players on
each side, it became rarer to kick the ball and more common to
carry or 'hug' it. In these circumstances, it was not surprising that
the game often degenerated into nothing more than a huge scrum.
When you consider that all this was going on in the main streets
of the town, the level of disruption can be imagined. Shops had to

close – in fact, shop assistants considered the day to be a holiday when they could take part in the game. The crush of the players could cause appreciable damage. Before the widespread use of thick plate glass for shop windows, the small panes set in wooden glazing bars could easily be caved in. Street lighting was vulnerable, too. The old oil lamps in their glass bowls and the newer gas lamps had to be protected from the flying balls by being wrapped in sacking.

Despite this disturbance to daily life, it is interesting to note that in the early part of the 19th century, Shrove Tuesday football was tolerated and even supported by leading tradesmen and local gentry. However, this was to change. Increasingly shopkeepers became reluctant to lose an afternoon's trade and the respectable classes distanced themselves from the anarchic mob. Local councils moved from supporting the game to attempting to put a stop to it, and with the introduction of police forces in the 1830s they had the means to do so. The game died hard in Kingston, however, but massive police reinforcements drafted in on Shrove Tuesday 1867 finally succeeded in bringing the tradition to an end. Similar scenes were repeated in other Surrey towns until only Dorking continued playing the game.

Dorking lies in the middle of the county, some distance from the main centres of Shrove Tuesday football nearer London. Perhaps this relative isolation played a part in maintaining the game longer than elsewhere. It seems to have first been played in Dorking in the 1830s, though it soon became a cherished tradition.

The day began with a group of bizarre figures in make-up and fancy dress parading through the town, carrying the balls to be used in the afternoon's games. Originally two, later three, balls were displayed on a cross-bar that bore the slogan *Wind and water's Dorking's glory*, perhaps a reference to the bad weather that was often a feature of the game. Musical accompaniment was provided by tin whistles and a drum, and sometimes a fiddler as well. They attempted to play 'the football tune', though not always with much success. A man dressed as a woman was the jester of the group, who exchanged banter with the people they encountered; sometimes the banter was a little too earthy for Victorian tastes. There was a serious purpose to all this. They carried a collecting box for contributions. The money was intended to pay for any damage that might be done during the afternoon's games; in practice, though, most was spent on drink in the pubs afterwards.

Soon after midday the shops were closed and the shutters put up over their vulnerable windows. The shop assistants themselves (who in those days were almost entirely young men) would often then join the crowd to watch or play the game. As the clock of St Martin's church struck two, the first ball was kicked off from the top of Church Passage. This was traditionally done by the town crier. Church Passage was the point where Dorking was divided between the two opposing teams: the Eastenders and the Westenders. Each tried to keep the ball in their own half of the town.

The first ball was known as the boy's ball, intended only for youngsters who would have found it hard to compete with grown men. An hour later, that game ended. Originally there were only two games, but at some point a third was introduced, the ball being kicked off at three. However, the game that really mattered started at five o'clock, when a large, gilded ball was kicked off. By this time the crowd had grown to several hundred, and play could be very rough. Duckings in the brook were a feature of the early history of the game, but had been abandoned by the 1870s. If the ball was carried into a pub, then play was suspended for a quick drink before the ball was thrown back into play from an upper window. Tension grew towards six o'clock, for whichever side held the ball in their territory when the church clock struck was the winner for the year. In fact, the Westenders nearly always won, simply because there were more people living in the western part of the town. A win for the Eastenders was rare: in 1866 this was only because they were reinforced by navvies building the London & Brighton Railway.

*Dorking High Street on Shrove Tuesday 1897, with the crowd of
football players (including one woman) surging after the ball.
A couple of policemen seem content to follow along.*

After six o'clock the town rapidly returned to normal. Many of
the players held a dinner at the Sun, which was the recognised
headquarters where compensation could be claimed for damages.
Any of the collection left after this was spent on alcoholic
refreshments. Perhaps not surprisingly, the Temperance movement
took an increasingly disapproving attitude to this custom. In the
years around 1890 they held a free tea party after the game as a
rival attraction to the demon drink. It did not seem to have the
desired effect, however: the players would gratefully drink the tea
and munch the buns – and then go to the pub.

The Dark Days: Winter and Lent

However, Shrove Tuesday football in Dorking was as surely doomed as in other Surrey towns. While respectable tradesmen were involved, it could continue as a proud local tradition. When the respectable classes withdrew, and tradesmen complained of loss of business, then the full force of Victorian law descended to snuff it out. Arrests and unexpectedly heavy fines in 1897 effectively put an end to the last surviving street football tradition in Surrey. There was no place for public disorder in the changing society of the county.

<hr/>

The day after Shrove Tuesday is Ash Wednesday, when in the Middle Ages the priest had marked the sign of the cross in ashes on the foreheads of the people kneeling before him as a reminder that they must come to dust and ashes. It was the first day of Lent and for six and a half weeks there was to be no celebration and an austere diet. After the Reformation the Protestant church did away with the symbolism of the ash, but the notion of fasting fitted well with Puritan self-denial.

Oddly, in some parts of Surrey the 'ash' of Ash Wednesday became associated with the tree of that name rather than the dust. It became the practice for schoolchildren to carry a twig of ash, either worn in a buttonhole or concealed in a pocket or sock. When challenged to 'Show us your ash!', it had to be produced or else a stamp on the toes could be expected. Like many similar customs, this was only enforced in the morning, and ceased to be valid at noon. This tradition was observed in Dorking, Godalming, Ewhurst and Hambledon well into the middle of the 20th century, but seems rare elsewhere. It has a lot in common with the custom of carrying oak leaves on the 29th of May and may have originated from it.

At Ewhurst it was the custom to sweep the fleas off the doorstep on 1st March, or otherwise the house would suffer fleas all the year. This symbolic sweeping had to be done before seven in the

morning to be effective, however. In other places, Candlemas had been the day for such ritualised spring-cleaning.

The fourth Sunday in Lent saw a relaxing of the strict Lenten fast, known as 'Pudding Pie Sunday' in Limpsfield. Some of the delicacies that had been given up could be indulged in on that day. The more usual name was 'Mothering Sunday', a tradition which seems to have spread from the western counties of England. The epistle in the Book of Common Prayer for that Sunday refers to the heavenly Jerusalem as 'the mother of us all', and this seems to have prompted the custom.

If a son or daughter no longer lived in the family home, it was traditional to pay a visit to their mother then. This was not a particularly difficult task if the child lived in or near the village in which they were brought up. In fact, a study of Surrey marriage registers shows that the majority of couples had previously lived less than ten miles apart in the mid 19th century. Married sons or daughters could thus probably have visited their mothers during the day. It was the unmarried girls who probably had the furthest to go. Many, perhaps most, farm workers' daughters became domestic servants in their teens. Many gravitated to London, where demand for servants was high and consequently so were wages. We can hope that some London employers at least were kind enough to allow their maid the two or three days' absence necessary to visit her mother deep in Surrey. We can be sure, however, that some were not.

The rainy winter months made travel difficult on the byways of Surrey. The main roads had become turnpikes in the 18th century, with gravel surfaces maintained from the tolls charged to road users. The minor roads or byways were a different matter. The

The windmill was a prominent feature of Ewhurst, a village where fleas were ritually swept off the doorstep on 1st March.

clay of the Weald and the Thames valley turned to sticky mud that could pull a shoe off an unlucky walker. The sandy soils south of the Downs were little better: rainwater eroded the lanes away so deeply that the road surface was far below the level of the surrounding land. These 'holloways' often had the gnarled roots of trees projecting from their banks as they had to stretch down further and further to seek nourishment from the infertile soil.

Often, Surrey lanes could become nothing more than streams of mud. To make their way along them, the country people would inch along the banks, clutching at roots and saplings to prevent themselves slipping into the mire. The story is told of a man working his way along a lane in this fashion when he spotted a fine hat lying in the mud. It was new, and too good to leave there, so he grabbed a branch and leant down to pick it up. To his astonishment, there was a head below it. 'Are you alright?' he asked. 'Yes, I'm alright,' replied the head, 'but I'm worried about my horse.'

Shepherds were busy with lambing, and towards the end of March special lamb markets were held in Guildford. These were an important part of the sheep-farmer's year over a wide area of

---

Mellersh Hill at Wonersh is typical of the deeply-cut 'holloways' of southern Surrey. They could become quagmires in winter.

Old Tanner, the shepherd at Hackhurst Farm, in the late 1890s.
His worn Surrey-type smock, round hat and gaiters
were already outdated by forty years or more.

Holmwood, where a farm labourer sang of the painful plough.

Surrey and north-east Hampshire. Flocks would be penned in sheepfolds made of hurdles bound to stakes, on the Fair Field on the Mount looking down on the High Street. The Fair Field, however, disappeared in 1885, when it was dug away to build the turntable engine sheds of the London & South Western Railway below.

On an arable farm the winter was the season for ploughing, breaking up the hard soil to produce a fine tilth for the sowing of the next year's crop. It was hard work, and celebrated in song. *The Painful Plough* was noted down from a carter in Holmwood in 1892, and Gertrude Jekyll knew of it in the Bramley area, where she thought it had been sung for a century or more:

> *Come all you jolly ploughmen of courage stout and bold,*
> *That labour all the winter in stormy winds and cold*
> *To clothe your fields with plenty, your farmyards to*
> *renew*

For to crown them with contentment behold the painful plough.

It is interesting to hear that the song rhymes 'plough' with 'renew'. In south-west Surrey 'trough' was pronounced 'tro'. It may well be that 'plough' was pronounced 'ploo'. Unfortunately, little was done to note down the Surrey dialect until it had almost vanished, and we cannot know for certain. There was a general feeling that Surrey did not have a true dialect, that Surrey English was standard English. This view was stated as early as 1589, when the author of *The Art of English Poesie* (who had the splendidly west Surrey name of George Puttenham) claimed that 'we of Middlesex and Surrey' spoke the pure and genuine English. Anyway, the song goes on to compare other occupations with that of the ploughman, and points out that all of them need to eat the bread that the plough provides.

I hope there's none offended with me for singing this,
For it was not intended for anything amiss.
If you consider rightly you'll own what I say's true:
There's no trade you can mention as can live without
the plough.

The Painful Plough is one of a common type of folk song known as a 'come all ye'. They are characterised by having a line of around 14 syllables and verses of two rhyming couplets. The long line makes it very easy to fit words to the tune, and it is not difficult to rhyme pairs of lines. Not surprisingly, the 'come all ye' was a popular song form, and takes its name from the opening line of the many versions that were composed to honour different callings.

Another Surrey song has grimmer origins. Winter was the season for foxhunting, and in January 1834 Barnard Hankey, Master of the Surrey Union hunt, rode out with his hounds. He was not prepared for what was to happen next:

A meet of the Surrey Union at the Royal Oak, Brockham in the early 20th century. Another meet, in 1834, led to a gruesome discovery.

It was Hankey the squire, as I have heard say,
Who rode out a-hunting on one Saturday.
They hunted all day, but nothing they found
But a poor murdered woman, laid on the cold ground.
About eight o'clock, boys, our dogs they throwed off
On Leatherhead Common and that was the spot;
They tried all the bushes, but nothing they found
But a poor murdered woman laid on the cold ground.

She was took off the common and down to some inn,
And the man that has kept it, his name is John Simms.
The coroner was sent for, the jury they joined

And soon they concluded and settled their mind.
Her coffin was brought; in it she was laid,
And took her to the churchyard that was called
Leatherhead.
No father, no mother, nor no friend I'm told
Come to see that poor creature put under the mould.

So now I'll conclude and finish my song,
And those that have done it, they will find themselves
wrong.
For the last day of judgement the trumpet will sound
And their soul not in heaven, I'm afraid, won't be found.

This episode must have had a great impact on local people at the time, and one of them was moved to commemorate it in this song. He was a brickmaker named Fairs, and he recorded the details in a matter-of-fact way – even to the name of the landlord of the Royal Oak. The tune he used was a powerful and gloomy one, well suited to the subject. It was still being sung sixty years later, when it was noted down from a farm worker at Milford.

CHAPTER 2

Renewal: Spring and Easter

S oon the fresh growth of the new season begins to appear, although cold weather can still be expected. The country folk called a cold spell, when thorn bushes were already sporting their blossom, a 'blackthorn winter'. The blossom can be late, however, even later than the arrival of the first cuckoo:

> *When the cuckoo comes to the bare thorn,*
> *Then there's like to be plenty of corn.*

This implied that a backward spring heralded a good harvest that year. The order in which trees came into bud was significant, too, in predicting the season's rainfall:

> *Oak before ash, have a splash.*
> *Ash before oak, have a soak!*

It was believed that whichever direction the wind was blowing from at noon on 21st March, it would blow from the same quarter for the following three months. Frederick Grover, a farm labourer near Farnham, recalled: 'Where the wind is at twelve o'clock on the 21st of March, there she'll bide for three months

St Thomas' church, Bourne. Frederick Grover of Bourne, near Farnham, was the source of much of the traditional lore noted down by George Sturt.

afterwards. I've noticed it a good many times, and sometimes it have come right and sometimes it haven't. But that old Dick Furlonger was the one. He said he'd noticed it hunderds o' times. We used to terrify 'n about that, afterwards 'cause he was a man not more 'n fifty!'

As at Candlemas, it was felt that unseasonably good weather had to be 'paid for' by bad weather later in the year:

> *So many mists in March you see,*
> *So many frosts in May will be.*

And,

> *If there's spring in winter and winter in spring,*
> *The year won't be good for anything.*

The first of April, then as now, was the day for fools, or 'gawks' as they were called in Surrey. The usual practical jokes were played on the innocent or unwary, such as being sent to fetch imaginary tools. A particularly time-wasting trick is noted from Dorking. A secret message would be entrusted to a lad to take to

St Michael's, Pirbright. The foolish villagers once tried to heighten the tower by piling manure around its base to make it grow.

Renewal: Spring and Easter

*The bleak and infertile landscape of Chobham Common
perhaps prompted the saying 'Two pairs of anything
would make a Chobham orchard'.*

someone, who would then send him on to another, and he to yet
another. The message? 'Send the fool farther!' Of course, all this
had to be perpetrated before midday. Any attempt to play a trick
after that drew the jibe,

*April Fool day's gone and past, so you're the greatest
fool at last.*

Stories told at another's expense have always been popular. One
tells of a postboy from the White Hart Inn on Guildford High
Street, who got lost one dark night on Winterfold Heath. As he
wandered about, he called out 'Lost! Lost!' A nearby owl hooted
'Who? Who?' 'Jack Penny, the postboy!' he replied.

Some Surrey villages had a reputation for stupidity. There was
a saying, *You don't have to go to Pirbright to find a fool.*

The villagers were said to run down to the stream when it rained, to drive the fish under the bridges to keep them dry. Pirbright was also credited with the most common of such tales, one told all over England, that the villagers attempted to rake the moon's reflection out of the pond. Chobham, too, was made the butt of jokes. *Two pairs of anything would make a Chobham orchard*, was a saying that probably referred to poor, arid soils of the heathland. Chobham was also credited with having treacle wells: another tale, like the moonrakers, told of many places.

It has to be said that Surrey folk were rarely complimentary about their neighbouring towns and villages. There are many rhymes which testify to local rivalry, such as,

> *Sutton for mutton,*
> *Carshalton for beeves,*
> *Epsom for whores*
> *And Ewell for thieves.*

or

> *Sutton for good mutton,*
> *Cheam for juicy beef,*
> *Croydon for a pretty girl*
> *And Mitcham for a thief.*

Before Victorian times, Guildford was the only town in Surrey with more than one parish church: it had three. The townspeople may have given themselves airs as a consequence:

> *Guildford, Guildford, proud people,*
> *Three churches and no steeple.*

In fact, Holy Trinity, at the top of the High Street, did have a steeple until 1740, when it fell, demolishing the church. The

Epsom's spa and horse racing may have attracted whores, but why Ewell was considered a den of thieves is hard to say.

rhyme must be a later invention. It may well have been chanted by Godalming folk, always great rivals of Guildford. It is unusual to find two market towns so close together, and a certain competitiveness is perhaps to be expected. Mary Tofts of Godalming claimed to have given birth to rabbits in 1726. This was soon proved to be a fraud, but the lads of Guildford were delighted. After that, they referred to any Godhelmian as a 'Godalming rabbit'. The answering retort was 'Guildford bull!' although the reason for this is now forgotten. The Godhelmians could console themselves by muttering the saying, 'Woking was, Guildford is, Godalming shall be'.

Another old adage may be old indeed. *The Vale of Holmes dale, never wonne, ne never shall* – a fragment of late medieval English,

---

Since the hoax of 1726, the people of Godalming were jeered at as 'rabbits' – at least by the youths of Guildford.

meaning 'The Vale of Holmesdale was never conquered and never will be'. This is said to be a reference to the Norman conquest, though there is no known historical basis for it.

One of the changes brought by the incomers to Surrey towards the end of Victoria's reign was the pronunciation of local place-names. For example, the old accent had pronounced Shalford as 'Sharfud' and Alfold as 'Arfud', practically rhyming them. This was to change, though, as the newcomers used the Standard English pronunciation of the written name. Burpham became 'Burfum' instead of the former 'Burp-hum', and Frensham was now 'Frenchum' instead of 'Fruns-hum'. (Oddly, nobody in London seems to have tried to change Clapham into 'Clayfum'.) It has been suggested that it was the introduction of the telephone which set the seal on this. The young lady operators who connected the calls had to be frightfully well-spoken, and naturally sounded the names of the exchanges as they were written. Nevertheless, there are people who continue to say 'Werpulsdun' for Worplesdon, 'Wunnersh' for Wonersh and 'Gumshul' for Gomshall, preserving a hint of the long-vanished local inflection.

The Sunday before Easter is known as Palm Sunday, commemorating Christ's triumphal entry into Jerusalem. In the Middle Ages, palm fronds were blessed in churches and carried in procession, a custom that was revived in many places during the 19th century. At Hascombe it was considered unlucky to have 'palm' in the house before Palm Sunday. Of course, genuine palm trees were virtually unknown in Surrey in those days, so as a substitute the blossom of the black willow was referred to as 'palm'.

Yew sprigs were occasionally used as an alternative 'palm', always green and readily available in the churchyard. There is a long-established belief that yew was grown in churchyards to provide wood for the long bows with which the village youths were required to practise. Its berries are dangerous to farm animals, so a graveyard might be considered a safe place for it to

These villagers gathered on East Shalford Lane, where Leman's Bridge crosses the Tillingbourne, probably called their village 'Sharfud'.

grow. On closer inspection (as so often) a more complex picture emerges. Medieval records show that yew staves for bows, rather than being home-grown, were imported in huge quantities. Moreover, sheep regularly grazed in churchyards to keep the grass down: some relatives even put up railings around family tombs to keep them out. It seems that the yew has a more ancient and symbolic role, associated perhaps with death and resurrection.

At Sherborne, in the parish of Albury, a fair was held on Palm Sunday with dancing and fiddling. This was put a stop to by the rector in 1810 or 1811, who transferred the festivities to May Day. One of the games was 'Tingling', a kind of mirror image of Blind Man's Buff. All the players were blindfolded except one, who carried a bell, which he had to keep 'tingling'. The players had to try to catch him, but if they got too close another man with a sack of sawdust would throw it under their feet to trip them.

RENEWAL: SPRING AND EASTER

It was believed that a loaf baked on Good Friday would keep at least a year and prevent sickness visiting the house during that time. In Limpsfield it was the custom to hang it up by a string. If a member of the household was struck down by an internal complaint, then a little of the loaf was grated into some gruel and fed to the sufferer. In 1889, one of these Good Friday loaves belonged to Mrs Mann, who lived in the Shambles, just off Guildford High Street. It had been old when her mother gave it to her 56 years before. From its description, it would seem to have been a hot cross bun, rather than a loaf. Such buns were, and still are of course, associated with the day.

In Cobham, Good Friday was the day to sow parsley, for it was said it would grow double what it would if planted on any other day. It was also a day for games. Quoits were rings of iron and the object of the game was to lob them at a stake, usually an iron rod. If they landed within half a yard of it they scored, but if a quoit 'ringed' the stake it scored much more. In fact, quoits were only a more elaborate form of horseshoes, which have been used for centuries in country districts in this simple game of skill. In the days when reading and writing were rare skills in a farming village, the score was kept by cutting notches in a stick or 'tally'. Indeed, this was the original way of keeping score at cricket as well.

Another Good Friday game was marbles, played seriously by men as much as boys. The usual game in southern Surrey involved shooting marbles to knock others out of a ring. The skill and tension of a good marbles match was every bit as exciting as modern snooker. A noted venue for marbles was the Greyhound Inn in Tinsley Green, just over the Sussex border. Here teams from Horley and Charlwood would play for the honour of their county on Good Friday each year.

It might be thought that playing games on the day which commemorated the Crucifixion was inappropriate. Indeed, there were those who thought so and said so. Perhaps the most dramatic example of this was the Good Friday dancing at St Martha's. In 1870 *The Times* described it in approving tones:

'A custom, the origin of which is lost in the obscurity of time, prevails in the neighbourhood of Guildford of making a pilgrimage to St Martha's (or Martyr's) Hill on Good Friday. Thither from all the countryside youths and maidens, old folks and children, betake themselves, and gathered together on one of the most beautiful spots in Surrey, in full sight of an old Norman church which crowns the summit of the hill, beguile the time with music and dancing. Whatever the origin of this pilgrimage to St Martha's, it is apparently one that commends itself to the taste of the present generation, and is not likely to die out with the lapse of years, but to increase in popular estimation as long as the green hill lasts to attract the worshippers of natural beauty, or to furnish the mere votaries of pleasure with the excuse and the opportunity for a pleasant holiday.'

St Martha's, one of the most isolated parish churches in Surrey, stood on a bare hilltop until trees began to cover it in the 20th century.

The Times seems to have got a little carried away by the Victorian myth of the 'Pilgrims' Way' in describing the dancing as a pilgrimage. Where the report was wrong, however, was in predicting that the gatherings would continue and increase in popularity. In fact, they would soon disappear, and leave only a few confused memories.

There is a suggestion that young people from Guildford actually danced to St Martha's, over Pewley Down. Others from Shere, Gomshall, Albury, Wonersh and other nearby parishes would join them. Crowds of over a thousand were estimated, many of them servant girls and male shop assistants. There would be gatherings at the top of the hill, but the main entertainment seems to have been on the flat ground at the foot, known as Bent Piece or Ben Piece. Here a small brass band, and a few fiddlers and accordian-players, would play for dancing, and games were played. The

St Martha's stands on the hill above Tyting Farm. At the foot of the hill is Bent Piece, where the Good Friday dancing took place.

Perhaps these children playing in the Tillingbourne downstream of Gomshall Mill would have attended the Good Friday dancing at St Martha's.

most popular of these games was 'Kiss in the Ring', to modern eyes a children's playground game but to young Victorians a rare chance to flirt and kiss. Indeed, the not-so-young Victorians seem also to have joined in with gusto. It was a time and a place where the crushing social conventions were suspended, where young men could approach young women for a dance and where 'persons of established reputation could galivant with rustic beauties'. Stalls were set up, selling nuts, sweets, oranges and ginger beer. All accounts agree that there was no alcohol on sale; there can have been few places in Surrey further from licensed premises. A sober and orderly occasion, then, and one of harmless pleasure. Sober and orderly it might have been, but some saw it as far from harmless.

Renewal: Spring and Easter

It was the Rev. Ernest Dugmore, curate of St Peter's, Vauxhall, who intervened in 1871. It is perhaps symbolic that it was a Londoner, rather than a local man, who tried to put a stop to the revels. Together with a group of gentlemen from Guildford, he distributed tracts urging a more solemn commemoration of Christ's death and burial. Later in the afternoon he held a short service with hymns in St Martha's church itself. All passed without incident. However, at this point Dugmore made a serious error of judgement. He led a procession down the hill, singing hymns and attempting to break up the festivities on Bent Piece. The *Surrey Gazette* reported: 'The indiscreet zeal on the part of the Rev. gentleman and his followers led to a most unseemly scene, in which the crowd completely mobbed them, assailing the party with most irreverent epithets, and pelting them with orange peel, turf and other things.'

Dugmore tried to address the crowd, but was hooted down and had to retreat once more to the church. The *Surrey Standard* took a more disapproving attitude towards this incident than the *Gazette*, and the *County Chronicle* suggested, 'Could not the day be changed, say to Easter Monday, and a programme of athletic sports arranged? Something might surely be done to render the day's holiday more enjoyable and more reputable than it is at present!'

As with Shrove Tuesday football, attitudes were changing and the Good Friday dancing declined rapidly. People still went to St Martha's on the day, but the dances and games were abandoned. By around 1900, only a single refreshment stall was put up and then that, too, vanished as the custom died.

Easter Saturday was considered a good day to sow seeds in the garden, 'while the Master's body lay in the ground'. The connection between Christ's resurrection and the seeds rising from the ground as if reborn was firmly fixed in the mind of the people

of Surrey; this despite the fact that the date of Easter varies by more than a month and has no link to the seasons. One possible explanation for this is simply that Easter Saturday was often observed as a holiday: most Saturdays were not. Those who wished to avoid working on the Lord's Day would otherwise have few hours of daylight to devote to their garden plots at that time of year.

Easter Day itself was a time for going to church. Together with the pub, the church was the focus of the village community, and it is not surprising that many stories were woven around the building itself. Perhaps the most common tale is that originally a church was to have been built in another place, but the morning after work had begun, the builders found to their astonishment that everything had been moved to a different spot. Each day it was the same: the day's construction was mysteriously relocated during the night. Some blamed the fairies or 'pharisees', others the Devil. Whichever supernatural power was responsible, however, eventually the builders had to give in and put the church up on the alternative site. Both Ewell and Haslemere were said to have no fewer than seven churches as a consequence. This story was often told to explain why a church stands at an inconvenient distance from the centre of the village, as at Dunsfold. Another origin of these tales could be that ploughmen, turning up tiles and other building materials, assumed that a church had once stood in that field. After all, what could such a substantial structure have been if not a church? In fact, these were traces of Roman villas, long forgotten but soon to be unearthed by archaeologists. Church Croft Knob at Puttenham and Church Field in Titsey probably owe their names to the remains of ancient buildings.

Eggs, of course, played an important part in the Easter celebrations. The tradition in Surrey as elsewhere was to colour hard-boiled hens' eggs with natural dyes. Onion skins were a favourite one, giving a rich reddish-brown which could be scratched from the shell to make patterns. From the 1870s, though, the moulded chocolate egg began to become more popular. The earlier tradition faded, but as late as 1935 the Model Dairy at Caterham was still sending dyed hens' eggs to its customers on Easter Day. Those who were acutely sensitive to the weather did not let a day of such importance pass without comment: *A fine Easter Day: plenty of grass, but little good hay*, implied that the late summer would be wet and the haymaking spoilt.

———◦⊙◦———

Easter Monday was sometimes marked by a custom known as 'Riding the Jack o' Lent'. This was recorded at Godalming as early as 1686, and was a way of mocking an unpopular local figure. In the early 1860s the following account was given of it at Haslemere.

'A custom prevails here on Easter Monday of riding a Jack o' Lent. It consists of setting up a figure on a stray horse, which is allowed to run about the town and is afterwards led from house to house and contributions levied, the boys shouting "Jack's up! Hurrah! Hurrah!" The figure is made to represent, as near as the garments at command will admit of the resemblance, some townsman who has offended the popular will. But it sometimes happens, when no delinquent can be found, the last newcomer has a ride (by no means a flattering welcome), or an old inhabitant, for no other reason than that he has never had a ride before. The custom is falling into disuse, which cannot be regretted, for very obvious reasons; but the writer remembers, soon after the last election in Haslemere, nearly a dozen mounted in the course of Easter Monday and the day following.'

Men were stationed in the roads on the outskirts of Haslemere to turn the horse back if it galloped towards them, and thus it was kept running back and forth throughout the town, accompanied by hundreds of cheering youths. The effigy had a placard round its neck which described the offence for which it was being paraded. It was then led from door to door and contributions collected. It was customary even to go to the house of the victim himself in this fashion, so that he knew of his public shame. Afterwards the effigy was hung or burnt as a fitting end for one who had 'broken the laws of society'. The offences specifically mentioned were wife beating and adultery, but the account above makes it clear that *somebody* had to ride in effigy each Easter Monday, even if there was nobody who had genuinely offended the townspeople. One year a local clergyman was picked on, for no good reason, and shamed the boys who brought his effigy to his door by giving them half a crown.

Haslemere High Street, where Jack O'Lent ran loose.

As with Shrove Tuesday football and other disorderly customs of the streets, Victorian respectability turned against the Jack o'Lent. Around 1849 the county police broke up the procession and tore the effigy to pieces. Those in favour of the tradition issued a poster mockingly offering a reward for the apprehension of those who had 'murdered' Jack o' Lent, and spoke out in the name of 'the children of John Bull' against a police force 'who are always on the alert to prevent and obstruct the inhabitants of this professed free country in their harmless amusements'. The authorities considered them far from harmless. One of the ringleaders prosecuted for the disturbance was fined the heavy sum of £5, which was quickly raised through contributions from other supporters. Nevertheless, subsequent Easter Mondays saw extra police drafted in to keep order. There were attempts to revive the Jack o' Lent, but the custom had died out by the end of the 1880s.

As ever, the coming of spring turned heads to thoughts of love, by far the most popular subject for traditional songs. While composed at some point by a jobbing wordsmith, and published in cheap booklets or broadsides, what made these songs 'traditional' was the process whereby they were passed from one illiterate person to another purely by ear. Naturally, a song in praise of farm workers could be expected to go down well with them. One such was noted down from a farm labourer in Dunsfold in the 1890s:

> *As I roved out one evening, being in the blooming spring,*
> *I heard a lovely damsel fair most grievously did sing,*
> *Saying 'Cruel were my parents that did me so annoy.*
> *They did not let me marry with my bonny labouring boy.*

Despite her parents' objection that he is beneath her station, the girl elopes and marries the boy. As one might expect and wish, they live happily ever after.

So fill your glasses to the brim, let the toast go round
Here's a health to every labouring boy that ploughs
and tills the ground,
For when his work is over, it's home he steers with joy,
And happy is the girl that gets a cheerful labouring
boy.

Birds played an important part in the folklore of spring. It was considered very lucky to see the first swallow or martin, and it was believed that swallows would bring with them from the distant seashore a pebble which had the power to restore sight to the blind. The cuckoo, however, was the most auspicious bird. On hearing the first cuckoo of spring, the Surrey folk would turn what money they had in their pocket over – so that it might be doubled.

The cuckoo has always been welcome as the herald of a warmer and brighter season. Mr Baker of High Field Farm, Thursley sang of her in 1913:

The cuckoo she's a merry bird, she sings as she flies;
She brings us good tidings and tells us no lies.
She sucks all small birds' eggs to make her voice clear
And she never sings 'cuckoo' till the summer draws
near.

CHAPTER 3

Holidays:
May Day and
Whitsuntide

O
f all the customs that have disappeared from our calendar, perhaps May Day is the most to be regretted. Once it was a time to celebrate the fresh growth of the warmer season with drinking, dancing and amorous flirtation. The first of May is now remembered, if at all, as something to do with international socialism or with children plaiting ribbons around a pole in the school playground.

In fact, the short school maypole is a relatively recent invention. The traditional maypoles of the past were usually tall and often permanently fixed. They served as the focus for merrymaking on May Day, when they were decorated with flower garlands. Dances were indeed performed around them, but these were circle dances, holding hands rather than plaiting ribbons. Churchwardens' accounts from all over Surrey show that maypoles were maintained by the village authorities; as indeed they should have been, for the May festivities were frequently fund-raising events for the parish.

Large permanent maypoles stood from Tudor times until the

18th century near Ham House, Petersham, the Apple Market in Kingston, in Croydon and at Chobham. The Guildford maypole stood at the junction of the London and Epsom roads, a massively tall, two-section structure with cross-trees like a ship's mast. It was such a prominent landmark that the road distances to and from Guildford were measured from its base. It remained standing until the 1840s, though by then the celebrations associated with it had long been abandoned. At Molesey in the 1840s the maypole was represented by a tree near the Bell Inn, around which the young people would dance. The only survivor of these permanent maypoles is on the green at Wood Street, in the parish of Worplesdon. This was standing there in 1828, but decayed away soon after. By then the dancing had been long forgotten. However, in 1871 some local gentry revived the custom by setting up a new maypole and organising a village sports day, including a cricket match. The pole has been maintained ever since, the present one being renewed to mark the Queen's coronation in 1953.

By the early 1800s, adults had largely given up celebrating May Day. The *Surrey Advertiser* commented in 1866, 'May Day and other old-fashioned celebrations have long ago come to be considered boorish and useless.' The first of May was left to the children. It became established as a rare day off for chimney sweeps' boys, whose usual trade was to climb up inside sooty chimneys with hand brushes and wooden shovels. John Mason of Guildford recalls that in the 1830s and 1840s,

> 'May Day was the chimney sweepers' holiday. Then they dressed in suits after the manner of a harlequin, tinselled and spangled in all the colours of the rainbow, and in groups of five or six performed their peculiar dance, beating out the tune to the music of the shovel and brush and triangle. Town houses and country mansions had to be visited and in some of the latter they were well entertained so that their revelry occupied at least a week.'

Holidays: May Day and Whitsuntide

George Sturt, the wheelwright, remembered May Day in Farnham in the early 1860s. 'On that same morning the chimney sweepers came round, gathering largess. A wonder it was to see that their oddly familiar faces, usually sooty, were really much the same colour as other people's. Their voices proved who they were, as they sang and danced, clattering their hand-brushes against their wooden shovels and one of them "playing the bones" held between his knuckles. They had come through from the street to our back yard – two or perhaps three half-grown lads, already crooked from overwork, and there in the forenoon sunlight they danced and clattered and sang.'

The popularity of the book *The Water Babies*, which told of the harsh life of a sweep's climbing boy, led in 1864 to a ban on sweeps employing boys. The tradition of their May Day dancing soon faded away.

It may be this same tradition that Finny noted from one old Kingstonian, who 'remembers when as a boy he and seven others, with "Jack in the Green" and a piper, who also beat a drum, dressed themselves up and went about the town "gigging" on May Day. They went from house to house and did simple traditional dances, which he learnt from the others.' 'Jack in the Green' was a familiar figure accompanying the sweep's boys. In effect, he was a walking – or dancing – bush, a bell-shaped wickerwork frame covered with green leaves with a man inside, whose face peered through a small hole left in the foliage. The sweeps' 'Jack in the Green' seems to have had its origins in London at the end of the Georgian period. As well as Kingston, it was seen in the streets of Mitcham, Chertsey, Croydon, and even Dorking. The simple, traditional dances may have been similar to the morris.

From Tudor times until the middle of Victoria's reign, Surrey had a strong local tradition of morris dancing. What set it apart from other forms of folk dancing was that it was for men only, rather than couples, and was a spectacle rather than something in which the onlookers could join. The morris probably had its

The Borough, Farnham. Until the early 1860s, this is where the chimney sweeps' boys would dance on May Day.

origins as part of court entertainments, which were copied and adopted first by town corporations, and then by the villages. Surrey, with its royal palaces at Richmond, Oatlands and Nonsuch, was perhaps the first county in England to feel its influence. In the days of Henry VII morris dancing became a prominent part of the fund-raising festivities for the parishes. The churchwardens' accounts of Kingston record income – and expenditure – on costume relating to the parish morris men. In 1530 Holy Trinity, Guildford was hiring out its morris gear.

There are few records of the morris in Surrey before the 19th century, although it seems to have continued as a feature of country celebrations. John Russell was selling morris bells from his shop in Guildford High Street in Georgian times, and around

HOLIDAYS: MAY DAY AND WHITSUNTIDE

1770 morris men from Compton regularly visited Losely House at Christmas. The first detailed account of the Surrey morris comes from the Rev. Francis Kerry, curate of Puttenham, in 1869:

'Puttenham like most other places had its morris dancers in former times – but none of the present generation remember having seen the performers with bells, as was the ancient practice. But Mr Fludder states that Thomas Furlonger his father's carter wore them in the dance, and that he was by far the best dancer in the whole neighbourhood, the bells on his legs and ankles keeping wonderful time with the musician.'

For the village children, 1st May became Garland Day. The custom was well described by James Thorne in 1844:

'During the last few days of April, the village children go about the meadows, and collecting all the cowslips they can find, form them into garlands, chaplets, &c., and on May-morning they assemble, and uniting in bands, carry their garlands, arranged commonly on two hoops crossed vertically and fixed on poles, about the neighbourhood ... last May-day we saw many of these little companies at as short a distance from London as Carshalton and Beddington.'

In 1891, the rector of Ockley also described the tradition, when it was already in decline:

'An old custom seems to be dying out, that of children bringing round garlands of flowers on May-day. It may be well for it to do so if ragged bunches of flowers tied to the end of a stick are made the only excuse for asking a penny. But time was when the flowers were arranged with a certain amount of art and beauty.'

Three or four loops covered lightly with green leaves and flowers, and linked together as a chain, or crossed and interlaced together in the shape of a globe, or a wreath or festoon hanging gracefully. These, if daintily made, were a pleasure to see, and a penny was readily forthcoming as a tribute of welcome to the evidences of a brighter and pleasanter time of the year.'

These garlands were carried from door to door, the children chanting a little rhyme. The usual version ran:

The First of May is Garland Day,
So please remember the garland
We only come here but once a year,
So please remember the garland.

In Victorian England, of course, 'Please remember' meant 'Please contribute to'. The pennies and halfpennies collected would be distributed among the children afterwards – often it would have been the most money they had at any time of the year. A lady in Limpsfield would regularly give a silver fourpence. A Dorking grocer would give a penny each for the garlands at the end of the day, and dozens could be seen decorating the shop front. Norman Wilkinson entertained over a thousand children to tea and plum cake on May morning on the lawn of his house at Redhill in the 1860s, giving each a threepenny bit. Until his death in the mid-1870s, the Guildford draper Thomas Horn always gave a penny and a printed cotton handkerchief to the children who brought garlands to his house in the Epsom road. The mercenary motive is perhaps a little too clear in the rhyme from Hambledon which brusquely went:

The First of May is Garland Day
Give me a penny and I'll go away.

*Children carrying garlands of the simple 'maypole' type on
Brockham Green, 1st May 1908. By that time, the custom
was fast disappearing. (Country Life)*

On Brockham Green in 1908 a group of village children was
photographed with their garlands. Since the invention of cameras,
Surrey photographers had concentrated on portraits or local
scenes. They did not usually bother to take pictures of the customs
of the rural poor. By 1908, however, cameras were becoming
widely-owned and garland-bearing was becoming rare enough to
be considered worth recording.

Garland-bearing used to be widespread in 19th century
England, and is still preserved in a few places. The decline of the
custom in Surrey can be linked with the rise of primary education.
The Education Act of 1870 established school places for every

child in the land, and soon every child was required to fill that place. May morning was not usually an official school holiday, and so any children who went absent carrying garlands were noted in the register. The school logbooks give a clear record of the decline of the custom as increasingly successful efforts were made to reduce truancy. Merrow school actually gave the children a half holiday, or even the whole day, until the mid-1880s. After that, 1st May was an ordinary school-day and truancy was recorded: in 1895, for example, 'Many of the poorer ones absent Maypoling'. This seems to confirm that the pennies collected were an important motive for the custom, and that the garlands themselves had become the flower-covered sticks known as 'maypoles'. At Abinger school the master recorded in 1900, 'For the first time during my 14 years as Master in charge of the school no child was absent going round 'maying'. The custom seems to have died a natural death.'

It is questionable whether the death of the custom was natural. The education authorities were anxious to reduce truancy and remodelled the celebrations into a school activity. The key figure in this process was the writer John Ruskin, who introduced a May Queen ceremony to the trainee teachers at Whitelands Training College in 1888. In many aspects of their artistic life, the Victorians showed a sentimental longing for the past. It is interesting to note that some local authors used the May festivities to evoke the spirit of a lost 'Merry England'. Both Albert Smith's *Blanche Heriot or the Legend of the Chertsey Curfew Bell* of 1842, and Martin Tupper's *Stephan Langton, a Romance of the Silent Pool'* of 1858 open with fanciful May Day scenes set in medieval Surrey. We have already seen how a May Day fair was instituted at Wood Street in 1871.

Ruskin was keen to revive May Day as a national festival, and saw the blossoming network of schools as a way of achieving this. He had heard of dancing round the maypole, and imagined the ribbon-plaiting dance of southern France to have been the same thing. He had heard of Queens of the May, and so his ceremony was to include the crowning of the May Queen. Ruskin's May Day was an immediate success and rapidly became established in schools throughout the country. It was introduced into the Girls' School in Dorking in 1904, at the same time that garland-bearing was dying out at the Boys' School. At Abinger the children still made garlands, but now they brought them to school to be judged by the vicar and his wife. Garlands were incorporated in the Bramley School May Day celebrations as late as the 1920s. Newdigate introduced the ribbon-plaiting maypole dance in 1910, and the crowning of the May Queen in 1931.

In Guildford, the last garlands seem to have been carried in 1905, and there are few records of them elsewhere after this date. Garlands continued in Albury until the First World War. They were carried by two girls in Forest Green as late as the Second World War, encouraged by their grandmother. They tied buttercups, daisies and grasses to a stick and took it from door to door. However, they did not collect any money.

As the children's garland-bearing disappeared from Guildford, 1906 saw the organisation of a May Day horse parade. Other towns instituted the same parade, in which tradesmen and carters were encouraged to decorate their horses with flowers and ribbons. The days of horse-drawn transport were quickly fading, however, and the horse parade did not really become an established tradition.

The sixth Thursday after Easter is Ascension Day, or 'Holy Thursday' as it was known. There was a belief that rainwater collected then would keep forever, rather like the bun or loaf baked on Good Friday. 'If you ketch'd the rain water as it fell on Holy Thursday, and put it in a bottle and corked it, you might keep it as long as you would, and it would never go bad.' Probably the water, like the loaf, was supposed to have healing powers.

The 29th of May was the anniversary of Charles II's restoration to the throne, and became a day on which to demonstrate loyalty to the crown. In pre-Victorian Dorking, as elsewhere, it was the custom to display a large bough of oak leaves on the church tower to commemorate Charles' hiding in an oak tree to escape from the Roundheads after the Battle of Worcester. This tradition survived in a modified form as late as the 1970s at Witley, where an oak branch was hung in the ringing chamber of the church tower on that day.

The association of the monarchy with the oak was maintained by the children on what they named Oak Apple Day or Shik Shak Day. An oak sprig, preferably with an oak-apple with it, had to be worn in the buttonhole on 29th May. Any who failed to do so would be called a 'shick-shacker' and could be kicked, stung with nettles or have their toes stamped on. At Ewhurst, as on April Fool's Day, this forfeit did not apply after midday. George Sturt recalled that in the 1860s some of the Farnham boys would carry their oak leaves concealed, only to be produced when challenged by others intent on punishing them.

Whitsun or Pentecost falls 50 days after Easter, and in Tudor and Stuart days it was a time for 'church ales': fund-raising events to meet parish expenses. The parish officials would brew ale and sell it at social evenings. These church ales could, perhaps naturally, become rather drunken affairs and were opposed by those of a Puritan disposition. They largely disappeared from Surrey in the 17th century. However, the large copper cauldron used at Frensham to brew for the church ales was parish property and is still in the church. Its original use forgotten, the cauldron became the focus of a local legend. There are many versions of the tale, some dating from Stuart times, but perhaps the most developed is one told by an old Farnham lady who learnt of it in Victoria's reign:

*All Saints, Witley, was the last church in Surrey to bring
oak leaves into the tower on Oak Apple Day.*

'Mother Ludlam was a witch and a herbalist and the
people came to her for help and potions, which she made
in a large cauldron. One day Mr Nick came and asked her
to lend him her cauldron. Mother Ludlam saw his foot
marks in the sand, those of a goat, and refused. While her
back was turned Mr Nick seized the cauldron and made
off with it. Mother Ludlam mounted her broomstick and
flew after him. The Devil had his seven league boots, and
fleeing from Mother Ludlam, made seven great leaps. At
each leap a hill arose, which are the Jumps. He left the
cauldron on the last and highest, called Kettlebury Hill,
and disappeared, forming the Devil's Punchbowl in the

side of Hindhead. Mother Ludlam picked up her cauldron and took it to Frensham church for safety.'

In fact, there are only three Jumps, rather than seven, but the tale is a classic example of legends woven around curious features of the landscape. There is a closer link between the Devil's Jumps and Whitsun festivities, for it used to be the custom for the people of Frensham and Thursley to have a picnic with dancing on the eastern, or Stony, Jump on Whit Tuesday.

Whit Monday was the usual day for such entertainments. It was often the day on which the village clubs and friendly societies would have their annual procession or walk, sometimes in elaborate regalia and accompanied by a band. There usually followed a communal dinner. This tradition was already waning by the 1860s, however.

Mother Ludlam's Cave at Moor Park can still be seen beside the footpath. It has lost its elaborate gates, however.

Holidays: May Day and Whitsuntide

Perhaps the most dramatic Whitsun custom was the annual fight between the boys of Ewhurst and the boys of Cranleigh. This took place at the Boy and Donkey Inn every Whit Monday. The details are a little confused, some saying the Ewhursters were known as the Roundheads and the Cranleigh lads were the Diamond Tops, others claiming different names, and even different locations. There is no doubt, however, of the tension between the youths of Cranleigh and the rough folk who lived in Hurtwood, the high ground between Ewhurst and Shere. The narrow lanes made the area almost inaccessible and it had a reputation as a refuge for poachers, smugglers and others beyond the law. The first policeman in Peaslake was appointed at the end of Victoria's reign, and his first task was to put an end to another annual fight between local youths and the boys of Gomshall.

The sandy hills known as the Devil's Jumps stand on Frensham Common. Today, however, the heathland around them has become more overgrown.

This kind of feud could be found in other places in Surrey. For example, the schoolboys of Warlingham and Whyteleafe fought out their rivalry in pitched battles, throwing turf in summer and snowballs in wintertime.

May was the most popular month for fairs. Of the 50 ancient fairs in Surrey, 16 were held in May (or at least they were when Easter was at its midpoint date of 8th April). There were none in January or March – possibly because of poor weather – though December, February and April had two each. The larger towns had their specialities, based on the agriculture of their market areas. Dorking was famous for poultry, with its local breed of

This blurred photograph of the mid 1860s shows a fair held in Guildford High Street. The audience for the Punch and Judy is all adult – including some farmworkers wearing smocks.

five-toed cocks. Farnham was noted for hops and corn, while Guildford's May fair was a fixture in the sheep farmers' year, as was Reigate's for cattle-breeders. The local fair was a great occasion, the servant girls and apprentices looking forward to them for weeks beforehand. In the morning the commercial business of the fair was carried out: cattle could be sold, horses bought and household goods purchased from the dozens of stalls. The afternoon and evening were for entertainment, with perhaps a bout of backswords in a ring, and always dancing. Fairs drew young people from many miles away, and provided the best opportunity for them to meet. Many marriages had their origins at the fair.

Fairs were also labour exchanges, where farmers could hire employees from those seeking work. Of course, the employer could be a bad one, and a song went round at Reigate hiring fair warning of a situation to be avoided. It is composed in the familiar 'come all ye' form:

> *Come all you jolly ploughing boys that whistle through the fair*
> *Beware of going to Sawyer who lives near Horley here,*
> *For he's the worst old master that we have ever saw:*
> *We ploughing boys have taken an oath we won't go there no more.*

Seeds were planted according to the dates of local fairs: runner beans on Crawley fair day, autumn cabbage on Blechingley fair, mangolds should be sown before the Guildford May fair, and so on.

> *'A swarm of bees in May is worth a load of hay,*
> *A swarm of bees in June is worth a silver spoon,*
> *But if it comes in July it is not worth a fly.'*

If a swarm departs from a hive and alights in a neighbour's garden before noon, then it is considered to belong still to the owner of the hive – only he must give the neighbour the first honeycomb produced thereafter. After midday, though, the swarm becomes the property of the neighbour himself.

One morning in May by chance I did rove,
I sat myself down by the side of a grove,
And there I did hear the sweet nightingale sing.
I never heard so sweet as the birds in the spring.

These smock-clad boys at Hascombe were expected to carry
firewood for the home. Their father wears the heavy
corduroy trousers of the mid-Victorian labourer.

*Children at Farncombe in the 1860s. They were not too young
to collect horse-droppings in a barrow. The new school
behind them would limit their time for play.*

*All on the green grass I sat myself down
Where the voice of the nightingale echoed around;
Don't you hear how she quivers the note? I declare
No music, no songster with her can compare.*

*Come all you young men, I'll have you draw near,
I pray you now heed me these words for to hear,
That when you're grown old you may have it to sing
That you never heard so sweet as the birds in the spring.*

The children of a farmworker's family would be expected to
help their parents from an early age. Boys aged eight or even
younger were sent out to tend animals or scare birds from the

newly-sown fields for sixpence a day. The girls would help their mothers in the laborious routine of cottage life, until they were old enough to become housemaids.

Children have an instinct for play, however, and play they did when the opportunity came their way. Toys were costly and few, though: hoops, spinning tops and marbles for the boys, skipping ropes and dolls for the girls (though these were usually of wood or rags – china dolls were for the wealthy). When children played, therefore, they usually played with each other. The kind of chasing games still to be seen in Surrey playgrounds were widespread. While now they are given up by the age of seven or eight, in old Surrey even 12-year-olds would continue to play them. Boys' games like 'cudgel' – a crude form of cricket, in which a short stick takes the place of a ball, a thick stick serves as a bat and shallow holes are the wickets – could be improvised without expensive equipment. Group games were popular with younger children. Some, like 'Oranges and Lemons', 'Nuts in May' and 'Looby Loo' are not entirely forgotten today.

Skipping games were well-established. A typical game involved a pair of girls turning the rope, while others waited to be called. They were called in by a rhyme. One ran:

> *Down in the valley where the green grass grows*
> *Dear little [girl's name] grows like a rose.*

The girl whose name has been called has to run in and begin skipping.

> *She grows and she grows, and she grows so sweet!*
> *Dear little [another girl's name] came along the street.*

Then the next girl named must run in and take the place of the first. This continues until all have had a turn.

There would soon be less time for playing, however, as the busiest time of the farming year was approaching.

CHAPTER 4

Warmth and Light: Midsummer to Autumn

Summer was a busy time on the farms of Surrey, and few communal celebrations interrupted the rhythm of work. It is notable that most calendar customs take place in the half of the year from November to the beginning of May, when there were more opportunities to take time away from the seasonal demands of making a living from the land.

Make hay while the sun shines is not merely a proverb, but was a fact of life for livestock farmers who owned meadows. Now the long, lush grass would be scythed and allowed to dry in the midsummer sunlight. Turned often with rakes, it would finally be carted and stacked to sustain the animals over the coming winter.

On the sheep farms, early June would be the time for shearing. The warm weather softens the natural grease in the sheep's fleece, causing the wool to rise. Then the shearing gangs would come round, their hand-shears clicking away as the bundled fleeces piled up. John Keene of Pit Farm, Thursley had a song to celebrate it:

O sheep shear is approaching that makes the farmer smile
To see his mutton a-roasting, his pots so merrily boil.
Here's strong beer, ale and cider, boys, at nights so merrily
bring,
O there's none so rare as can compare with a farmer in
those things.

The song was, no doubt, one sung at the dinner traditionally given by the farmer to the shearers at the end of their labours.

The feast of St John the Baptist falls on 24th June, and the evening before is nearly the shortest night of the year. It was the time for St John's Vigil, or watching on St John's Eve. Francis Kerry, Curate of Puttenham in 1869 describes the custom as it was observed perhaps a century earlier: 'It was believed that if anyone sat up fasting all night in the church porch he would see the spirits of those who were to die in the parish during the ensuing twelve months come and knock at the church door in the order and succession in which they were to die.'

On one occasion a certain number of the villagers of Puttenham arranged themselves in the porch, the men on one side, and the women on the other. They 'awaited the hour of midnight when they saw all those who would be buried within the twelvemonth pass before them – among the rest, a handsome little girl, who playfully danced on her grave, and still more, the figure of one of the young men in the porch, who unfortunately was not able to keep awake – so necessary a precaution since the sleeper always appears in the sad procession. Singularly enough, the child died not long after, and this had such an effect on the young man, that he spent the remainder of the year in preparation for death, devoting his time to prayer and religious exercises'.

St Swithin's Day, 15th July, is famously a time for weather prediction. It is still widely believed that rain on that day means rain for 40 days thereafter. In old Surrey, St Swithin had a somewhat different significance. An old lady told A.J. Munby of Pyrford in 1881, 'We must have some rain tomorrow, sir, to christen the apples.' 'What is that?' asked Munby. 'Why, they always say, if there's no rain on St Swithin's Day, the apples don't get christened, and then they comes to nothing.' At Dorking, it was held that the nuts, too, were similarly baptised.

We have already noted the almost obsessional interest in foretelling the weather, and we must excuse this very English preoccupation. After all, this country has one of the most variable weather patterns of any in Europe, the successive fronts coming in from the Atlantic bringing constant change – and much rain. We grumble at this, but it is the high annual rainfall which made it possible to farm even the unpromising soils of Surrey. Even so, too little rain; too much; too early in the season or too late: all could make the difference between a good crop and a healthy flock – or otherwise. It is no wonder that proverbs, rhymes and superstitions surrounded the dark art of weather forecasting.

'If in summer moles forsake their trenches and creep about on the surface of the ground, it is a sign of hot weather; but if by chance they forsake the valleys and take to the high ground it is a sign of floods.' Moles were believed to be sensitive animals and were said never to burrow on Ockley Green, where legend recalls a dreadful battle anciently fought between the English and the Danes.

The phases of the moon were considered to be influential in affecting the weather. Many old eight-day clocks (or 'grandfather clocks' as they are now called) had a dial showing the phases of the moon. This was because the exact time that one phase changed to another was an indication of the weather to come. One old farm labourer near Reigate opined, 'I reckon we'll have a change afore very long, measter. I don't like the leuk o' the moon. She's a-lyin' a deal too much on her back.'

In passing, it should be mentioned that perhaps the most enigmatic crop prediction comes from Farnham. On 25th July they would say,

> 'Til St James's day is come and gone,
> There may be hops or there may be none.

Mitcham fair was held on 12th August and was associated with the children's custom of making 'grottoes'. The early Victorian grottoes were hollow pyramids of oyster shells constructed on the pavement, with candles inside them. By 1895, one near Mitcham Common was described as 'merely a conical mud heap, about two feet high, having large stones embedded in its surface, and a sprig of green stuck on the top'. The children would stand beside their grottoes, begging pennies from passers-by. One rhyme went:

Harvesting lavender at Carshalton in the late 1890s.
It seems to have been men's work.

Please remember the grotto: it's only once a year;
Please give me a ha'penny to spend at Mitcham Fair.
Father's gone to sea; mother's gone to fetch him back,
So please remember me.

My hands are so dirty, my face is so clean,
I've got a little pocket, to put a penny in.
A ha'penny won't hurt you, a penny won't kill you,
Tuppence won't put you in the workhouse.
My, my, happy day. Give me a ha'penny and I'll run away.

There are echoes of the May garlands in this custom, a suburban equivalent perhaps. Like so much else, it disappeared at the outbreak of the First World War. It was revived around 1950, however, with arrangements of stones, shells and flowers on the pavement. 'Grotter Day' was then in July, and the link to the former fair day seems to have been lost. It finally died out in the mid-1960s.

Summertime in Mitcham was the time to harvest the lavender, for which the parish had a great reputation. From the mid-18th until the mid-19th century large quantities were grown to be distilled into oil of lavender. It was also sold by hawkers in the street, with a song to advertise it:

Come all you young ladies and make no delay
I gathered my lavender fresh from Mitcham today.
Will you buy my sweet blooming lavender
There are sixteen dark blue bunches a penny.
You buy it once, you buy it twice
It will make your clothes smell sweet and nice.
Now's the time to scent your clothes and pocket
handkerchiefs
And keep the moths from your clothing.
Will you buy my sweet blooming lavender
There are sixteen dark blue bunches a penny.
Some are large and some are small

Please take them in and show them all
There are sixteen dark blue bunches a penny.

The Mitcham, Wallington and Carshalton area was full of market gardens. Here the 'simplers' or herb-growers would cultivate plants with medicinal powers. These they hawked about in baskets, crying out their wares:

> *Here's pennyroyal and marigold,*
> *Here's watercress and scurvy-grass.*
> *Come buy my wormwood and mugwort,*
> *Here's southernwood that's very good,*
> *Dandelion and house-leek.*
> *Here's dragon's tongue and wood seller,*
> *With boar's foot and horehound.*

Southernwood, also called lad's love or old man, was used to keep moths away from stored clothes. Horehound made a syrup for coughs and colds, and could flavour a cooling drink in summer. This was not folk medicine in the strict sense, in that no magical or ritual elements were involved in such herbal cures. Indeed, it was to these 'simples', or time-honoured recipes, that the qualified doctors and apothecaries turned for the ingredients of their remedies. The learned John Evelyn of Wotton had published *Sylva, or a Discourse of Forest Trees* in 1679 and included the healing properties of the various trees. The oak, so plentiful as to be known as the Surrey weed, could cure many ailments. Indeed, Evelyn asserted that 'the very shade of this tree is so wholesome, that the sleeping or lying under it becomes a present remedy to paralytics'. Furthermore, walnut leaves distilled with honey and urine 'makes hair spring on bald heads'. He reserved his highest praise, though, for the juniper and its berries. A syrup made from them would cure almost anything, a panacea, in fact.

Midsummer to Autumn

The summer moonlight was the time for the fairies to dance. The peculiar double plural of the old Surrey dialect named them the 'fairieses', and as that sounded much like the 'pharisees' of the Bible, then the pharisees they were. Like countrymen everywhere, the people of old Surrey believed in the little folk. They came from a supernatural world different from both Heaven and Hell, and just like angels and devils they could intervene on occasion in the lives of mortals.

The most common way they would annoy people was by riding their horses at night. Typically the carter or the ploughman would unlock the stable early in the morning – for stables were always locked, as horses were valuable – and there he would find them tired, sweating and panting in their stalls. Some might say these were just the common symptoms of a fever, but he knew better. As an old man at Tanhurst in Horley insisted, the pharisees had been magically riding them in the night. He would check their manes, as the pharisees would tie knots in the hair to act as stirrups. Tangles were sure to be found as confirmation. So the horseman would take steps to protect his animals. Perhaps a flint with a natural perforation in it would be hung over the horse's stall – the stone should be found, not given or bought, and a red ribbon used. Best, though, was iron, always a powerful defence against the supernatural. A sickle blade nailed to the manger, or a horseshoe nailed on the door would deter the pharisees. Horseshoes are still often nailed over stable doors in Surrey. When asked why, the usual reply is 'for luck'. In truth, the tradition has its origins in a very specific kind of luck: keeping the pharisees away.

The pharisees were not always a hindrance to mortal folk. If the whim took them, the 'good people' might help. In the summer season, they might mow the hay at night and leave it neatly in rows to be found drying in the morning sun. At least, this was the explanation given out on farms where a son may have deserted from the army or navy and returned home. He would have to stay hidden from the authorities, but equally he had to earn his keep. Not surprisingly, it was said to be

unlucky to spy on the pharisees at their night-time work. A cautionary tale was told to Francis Kerry, curate of Puttenham, in 1869:

> 'A farm servant was employed to thresh wheat in his master's barn, but every morning to his great surprise he found that a considerable quantity had been knocked out during the night. His curiosity was roused, so he resolved to discover, if possible, his mysterious assistants. Having seated himself one night on a beam in the mow [the side of the barn where the unthreshed sheaves were stacked], after a while he saw two diminutive beings enter the barn and seize each of them a flail. To work they went for a considerable time: at length one of them, pausing, said to the other, "I sweat; do you?" upon which the man shouted from his beam, "And the d...l sweat both of you!" They vanished instantly; and from that very night the fairies never again visited the barn.'

When everyone in the house was asleep, the pharisees might fly in through the keyhole and sport among the dying embers of the log fire. This was in the large, wide, open fireplace which modern estate agents call an 'inglenook' and which the people of Surrey called a down hearth. They expected to find it neatly swept, with a basin of water left for them. If so, in the morning the basin would be found empty with a silver sixpence in it. On the other hand, if the hearth, the very focus of the home, was left neglected, then upstairs they would fly and pinch the lazy servants black and blue as they slept.

───◦◦◦───

'Crack Nut Sunday' was the name given to the Sunday before Michaelmas at Kingston-upon-Thames. This referred to the curious custom of the parishioners cracking and eating nuts during the church service on that day. 'The custom was not restrained to the junior branches of the congregation, but was practised alike by young and old; and the cracking noise was often so powerful, that the minister was obliged to suspend his reading or discourse, until greater quietness was obtained.'

This may have had its origin in the annual Michaelmas feast accompanying the choosing of a new bailiff of the corporation. As can be imagined, the more reverential attitude towards religion that developed in the 19th century viewed this kind of behaviour in church with increasing disapproval. It seems to have lingered on, however, until the early years of Victoria's reign. Perhaps the local government reorganisation of 1835, which did away with the Michaelmas election, contributed to the decline of Crack Nut Sunday.

<hr />

Michaelmas, the 29th of September, was one of the quarter days, and consequently a common time for farm servants and others to seek new employment. Leatherhead used to hold a Michaelmas fair on the 29th until the change of the calendar in 1752, when eleven days were skipped to bring the British calendar into line with the Continent. This caused immediate problems for those who had been hired for a full year the previous Michaelmas. Were they expected to work another eleven days? Were they to be paid for a full year if they did not? The simple solution was to ignore the change completely, and Leatherhead fair was then held on 'old' Michaelmas Day, 10th October. In fact, many Surrey fairs adopted this practice, shifting their dates eleven days back as if the calendar change had never happened.

In Surrey, as elsewhere, it was traditional to eat goose at Michaelmas. A more local custom, though, was the Michaelmas loaf. 'On Michaelmas Day the eldest woman member of a family made a huge loaf of bread, but as it frequently happened that she

All Saints, Kingston, where the cracking of nuts on the Sunday before Michaelmas could drown out the preacher.

*In the background of this photograph of St Catherine's chapel can be
seen a frame for swings at the St Catherine's Hill fair.*

was very decrepit, the eldest man in the family was allowed to help
her. In the evening every member of the family collected in a room
and the bread was cut into equal proportions, so that each man,
woman and child should cut a slice, and have good luck for the
year. A married couple, if they desired an increase in their family,
could cut their portions in halves and throw one half to the birds.'

Some said it was at Michaelmas that the Devil claimed the
remaining blackberries as his own, others said it was 1st October.
From then on they must not be picked and eaten, for their
sweetness had gone and they were the Devil's fruit.

St Catherine's Hill stands a mile south of Guildford, topped by
a ruined chapel. A mile to the east, St Martha's church stands

This engraving of the fair on St Catherine's Hill dates from about 1830. In the middle distance, the crowd watching a cudgel match block a stagecoach approaching from Portsmouth.

similarly isolated on another sandy hill. Legend has linked the two by telling that they were built at the same time by two giant sisters – named Catherine and Martha, naturally. These giantesses had only one hammer between them, however, and when one needed it, the other would throw it across from one hilltop to the other. (The old lady who told me this tale added, 'And that's why people in Guildford have flat heads.')

In fact, St Catherine's chapel was built by the rector of St Nicholas' church in Guildford in the early 14th century. In return for this, he was given the right to hold a fair on the hill on 21st September and the four days following. By the time of the calendar change in 1752, the fair lasted only two days, but these were simply put back eleven days and thus held in October.

St Catherine's fair attracted crowds from far away. The Sunday before the fair was known as 'Tap Up Sunday', when the villagers of St Catherine's had the right to sell home-brewed beer at their cottage doors. The landlords of the local pubs were similarly absolved from the usual restrictions of the licensing laws. There grew up a curious tradition, whereby local people threw conkers at passers-by on the Portsmouth road. This seems to have been tolerated with good humour until 1863, when a larger than usual mob gathered. They not only pelted travellers with conkers, but with stones, and they manhandled and insulted them into the bargain. The disorderly crowd then built a bonfire, which prompted the suspicion that they were no other than the notorious Guildford Guys, whose annual riots on 5th November were getting out of hand.

An isolated farmstead in Highcomb Bottom, as the Devil's Punchbowl was officially called. Baring-Gould's novel The Broomsquire *was set here.*

Guildford housewives would clean their houses specially 'for the fair', and many took the date as the time to light the first fires in the hearth and would keep them burning until the next Guildford fair in May. The first day of the 'Katern' Hill fair was for business, when local brewers came to buy hops from Farnham and nearby. There were also stalls selling crockery and other household wares. The second day was for entertainment. There were booths selling drink, and large tents for dancing. Turner, the artist, depicted the fair around 1830, with singlestick or backsword players in action. This was a sport in which two opponents tried to hit each other's head with an ash stick, their knuckles protected by a basket guard. Whoever drew blood from the other's forehead which ran an inch was deemed the winner. The usual prize was a new hat. Enthusiastic crowds cheered the challengers on; a chance for local farm lads to prove their courage publicly. The particular delicacy of the fair was fried sausages served with watery 'Katern' Hill mustard.

However, the St Catherine's Hill fair, like many another throughout the land, declined during Victoria's reign. Social attitudes were changing, and the robust rustic entertainment of the fair was increasingly looked down upon as coarse and vulgar by the gentry, who had previously seen nothing wrong in joining in. Drunkenness and disorder, even brawls between gangs of local youths and gypsies, contributed to the disapproval of the better classes. By the early years of the 20th century it had lost a good deal of its former vigour, with merely a few stalls and fairground rides that disappeared as world war changed Old England forever.

The sterile heathland around Thursley and Hindhead afforded a hard-earned living to a few. These were the broomsquires, or broomsquarers. They made their brooms of birch or heather, binding the sprays into a tight bunch with strips of willow or hazel, and fastening them to the handle with a wooden peg. The brooms were sold for a few pence, and indeed the materials had cost the broomsquire nothing.

A gruesome murder in 1786 brought notoriety to Hindhead, then one of the most desolate spots in Surrey. As with the

The Red Lion, Thursley, on what was the main Portsmouth Road in the 1780s. Here the unsuspecting sailor met his murderers.

poor murdered woman of Leatherhead, the deed was commemorated in a song, which was sung among the gypsies until fairly recently.

> *Three sailors to the road lane* [the Red Lion, Thursley]
> *came,*
> *Lonegan, Marshall and Casey by name,*
> *They told a tale they were quite hard up,*
> *'Twas long since they had bite or sup,*
> *And they walked all night and day*
> *Yet Portsmouth town was miles away.*

*Beside the road through the deserted heathland of Hindhead stands
the stone commemorating a brutal and treacherous murder.*

Another sailor came along,
A smart young tar his name unknown,
Said, 'Cheer up, mates, don't be cast down,
For I'm going home to Portsmouth town.
As you have no cash the charge to meet
I've shot in my locker, and I'll stand treat.
He treated them with a right good will.
And they went together on Hindhead hill.

They reached the Hindhead hills at last;
Amidst the heath and purple grass,
That lad's blood – more purple real
Soon was flowing down the Hindhead hill.
Lonegan and Casey used the knife,
Marshall begged them to spare his life,
But his prayer did not avail,
That is as Marshall told the tale.

The deed was done! They dragged along
The body in the Punch Bowl flung,
The knife was cleaned, the stain wiped out,
They thought all trace removed, no doubt;
And long before the body found,
They'd be at sea and outward bound

Their complacency was misplaced, however. The murder had been witnessed, and a group of Thursley villagers pursued the three killers and arrested them. They were tried at the assizes and sentenced to death. They were hanged at the top of Hindhead, and their bodies then soaked in tar and riveted into iron frames. They were then suspended by chains on a gibbet, a high wooden post with an iron wheel at the top from which the three corpses swung in the wind as a warning to other wrongdoers passing on the road below. The unknown sailor was buried in Thursley churchyard, with a fine gravestone. On the site of the foul deed on the wild hillside of Hindhead, superstition has it that no heather or grass will ever grow.

CHAPTER 5

Harvests and Bonfires: The Fall of the Year

Harvest was the busiest time of the year on an arable farm, and the whole community was involved in the process of bringing in the crop of wheat, barley, oats or rye. Families would work together in the fields of ripened corn.

Typically, the husband would be one of a row of men, advancing in line across the field and cutting the stalks with a cranked sickle known as a hook. (Scythes were usually used only for cutting hay, not corn.) The hook would be held in the right hand and a short, bent stick known as a crook held in the left. Bending low, the man would pass the crook round a bunch of stalks and simultaneously cut them with the hook. Then by pulling the crook round to his left, he would lay the swathe behind him. He was then ready for the next cut, and so he would continue by hook and by crook. The wife might follow him, gathering the swathes into sheaves, binding them in the middle and propping several sheaves up into stooks. This kept the ears off the damp ground, and so prevented moulds or rot. Even the children could help and some village schools, at least in their earlier days, allowed a holiday for the

HARVESTS AND BONFIRES

Harvest at Frensham. (Rural Life Museum)

harvest. There was often only a short opportunity between the crop ripening and the bad weather that might flatten it or cause it to rot. As well as local labour, the farmer might employ itinerant harvest gangs, who followed the ripening corn from the south to the north of the country. Every scrap of daylight was used, and the harvesters might work under the light of the moon if it was full enough.

Around Farnham, the harvest was the hop-picking. Farnham hops were highly prized by brewers for their aroma and flavour, and regularly fetched higher prices than those of Kent and elsewhere. The soils were ideal, and careful choice of the time for picking contributed to a high-quality crop. The traditional way of growing hops was to plant them in small mounds of earth or 'hills', with poles stuck into them around which the hops climbed. The modern technique of wires and string was basically a 20th century innovation.

A correspondent described the beginning of the hop picking in early September, 1807. He met waggon-loads of people: 'These consisted mostly of the female sex, of all ages, collected from Hampshire, Berkshire, and other districts, and proceeding to the hop-picking at Farnham. It seems it is the custom for the growers to make musters of people in the villages, who assemble at an appointed place and time, when waggons are sent for their conveyance. The drivers of these living cargoes had their hats decorated with ribbons, and flags were placed in the front of the vehicles ... The best dressed girls were seated in the front, singing in full chorus ... We soon proceeded to a large plantation above the town, at which the picking was just commenced. ... a numerous band of pickers was ranged, divided into groups, each seated round great baskets, into which the women and children were pulling the hops, as they were brought clinging to the poles by men ... It was a lively and picturesque scene.'

The parson was, of course, entitled to a 'tithe' or tenth of the hops in his parish, as he was entitled to a tenth of all crops. These tithes were understandably resented. Some hop growers would 'compound' or give a cash payment, others would simply hand over a tenth of the hops picked. Knight of Farnham had a different approach. He left every tenth 'hill', or mound, unpicked for the Rector of Farnham to pick himself. The rector took him to court, but Knight won his case. The story is celebrated in *Farnham's Glory, a new song composed by Black Dick the Tinker*:

You hop-planters all, I pray now attend.
Unto these few lines here that I have pen'd
It is on a law-suit, will give you delight,
The Rector of Farnham against Mr Knight.

Many hop-planters here for their tithes did compound
And paid a great price for an acre of ground;
While others did pick them and gave them in kind,
But Mr J. Knight he was not of that mind.

Young women and girls pick the ripe hop blossoms from the bines twined round the hop poles, probably in the 1880s. The full baskets would be emptied into a cart after being tallied or credited to the pickers. (Jim Tice)

For every tenth hill he left as we find,
That the tithe-men might come and take it in kind;
But the hops was not pick'd as I have heard say
For they hung on the poles 'til they all blew away.

The song goes on to celebrate the judgement at Guildford Assizes in Knight's favour.

Farnham hops were often sold at Weyhill fair, on 10th October each year. The trusting countryman could become the victim of swindlers, however. Frederick Grover of Farnham recalled how Joey Ward was conned. 'Oh, ther' was two gentleman-looking chaps met 'n in the fair, an' one of 'em says, "Look, here's a 'ardworkin', industrious-lookin' man. If you can show me as much of

---

South Warren Farm at harvest time. In the background rises the wooded hill known as the Chantries. The barn is full, and both haystacks and cornstacks have been made to store the surplus.

your own earning, my man," he says, "I'll give ye a fi'-pun' note." Well, of course he very soon run off an' got what he'd jest took for he's hops. An' so there they got, tuckin' of'n up and tyin' up his pockets so's he shouldn't be robbed gwine 'ome. An' when he got 'ome, 'stead o' twenty sovereigns what he ought to ha' had; he pulled out twenty fardins.' The con-men had switched his gold sovereigns for copper farthings while pretending to examine them, and had carefully tied them into his pockets so that he would not discover the cheat until they were long gone. Some Farnham folk said that no fires should be lit to warm the house until Weyhill Fair – but 10th October seems rather late to do so.

After the harvest was gathered in, the farmer would traditionally give all the harvest workers a supper, the Harvest Home. The afternoon beforehand, a cricket match was sometimes played. Then benches and tables were set for the dozens of labourers in a farmyard or outbuilding; not in the barn, of course, for that was full. Apart from Christmas, this was probably the only time of the year when the Surrey farmworker had more than enough to eat. The menu was always the same: roast beef and plum pudding, with rather more beer than they really needed. Often the female members of the harvest gang would retire after the meal, to leave their menfolk to merrymaking. This always included songs, and a toast to the health of their employer.

The *Surrey Advertiser* reported in 1864, 'On Saturday afternoon "harvest home" was celebrated at Broadwater, when the whole of the men in the employ of Mr Murray Marshall were entertained with a sumptuous repast. The supper took place in one of the sheds attached to the farm buildings, about 180 sat down to partake of it. The chair was taken by Mr Marshall himself, and with the abundance of good cheer provided the greatest harmony and geniality prevailed. Some excellent songs were sung and toasts drank, not forgetting that of the worthy and much respected host, whose hearty and long continued health was pledged in a full bumper. The meeting was in every respect an agreeable one, as showing the good feeling which exists between master and man;

and so hearty was the enjoyment of all, that it was not till near midnight that the party broke up.'

The bond between master and men, which the harvest supper reinforced, became more strained as the agricultural depression set in. In 1874, agricultural trade unions were gaining membership as the farmworkers' standard of living declined. At Hoppingwood Farm near Kingston that year, Mr Horlick, the farmer, said at the harvest home that 'he thought his men would not want to throw their money away in joining any such unions. Good men were always sure to find good masters.' The evening ended when everyone in the company had sung a song.

Every man and every master knew dozens of songs suitable for the occasion. A typical one was *Harvest Home*. This version may

Fields near Redhill, where Daniel Gumbrill and his kind would have worked hard and celebrated the harvest with song.

have been collected from Daniel Gumbrill, a farmworker near Redhill, who was born in 1827:

Here's a health unto our measter, the founder of this feast,
I pray to God with all my heart his soul in heaven may rest.
That all his works may prosper, what'er he takes in hand,
For we are all his servants and all at his command.
So drink, boys, drink!
And see that you do not spill,
For if you do, you shall drink two,
For it is our measter's will.

Indeed, the drinkers would have to drink another toast if they spilt a drop. Another drinking game was 'I've been to France'. This involved the drinker holding a wooden bowl upside down and balancing a horn beaker of beer on its base. As the others sang, he had to empty the beaker without touching it with his hands, and then toss it into the air as he turned the bowl the right way up to catch it as it fell.

I've been to France and I've been to Dover,
I've been a-roving all the world over,
Over, over, over and over,
Drink up your liquor and turn the bowl over.
Over, over, over and over,
The liquor's all drunk and the bowl is turned over.

One imagines that as the evening progressed there was less of the liquor drunk and more spilt over the drinker and the company around him. A harvest supper song from Thursley sums up the spirit of the evening:

*Now master's corn is in the barn, all free from wind
and weather,
We'll all have a jolly good supper and we'll all sit
down together.
We'll drink our master's health, and all of us will keep
sober.
And when we've done
We'll laugh for fun,
And the month was called October.*

However, the reference to keeping sober may not have been realistic. Certainly, as the Victorian age wore on, the temperance movement increasingly tried to re-model the old Harvest Home into a teetotal occasion. The Baptists, in particular, took a lead in denouncing the excessive drinking, and attempted to replace the old dinner with songs by a tea-party with prayers. At Wonersh in 1864, for example, the Harvest Home given by Mr Colebrook of Tangley Farm consisted of tea served in a barn 'fitted up for the purpose of holding religious services', followed by sermons. At Grange Farm, Seale, the celebrations regularly included a corn-pitching contest between beer drinkers and abstainers. The two teams raced each other to load a waggon with sheaves. The beer drinkers seem always to have won. However, there was a practical as well as a moral justification for discouraging alcohol. Increasingly, machinery was being used on farms and especially at harvest-time. Steam-driven belts and unguarded cogwheels were a danger to a man under the influence of drink.

For reasons of safety, the loose smock or 'round frock', which had been the distinctive dress of the Surrey farmworker, was gradually abandoned. The Surrey round frock was of plain but finely-stitched linen. The design shows that it had developed from the standard pattern of a 17th or 18th century man's shirt, by simply becoming fuller and made of heavier material. It had small areas of smocking on either side of the neck opening, the shoulders and wrists, and a little embroidery on the shoulder

*The Harvest Home at Tangley Farm, Wonersh in the 1860s
had a religious and Temperance character, unlike the
beery revels still enjoyed elsewhere.*

straps. It lacked the deep smocking over the chest and the elaborate panels of embroidery found in other counties. The round frock would protect the labourer's clothes – always difficult to clean and expensive to replace – while allowing him free movement to work. At a time when few villagers could afford 'Sunday best', a clean white smock and a top hat were considered quite suitable clothes in which to go to church.

The round frock began to disappear from the 1860s. It was liable to be caught in farm machinery, often causing severe injuries to the wearer. Moreover, the rising tide of Victorian snobbery made a farm labourer increasingly reluctant to wear a garment that marked him out as a peasant. When Lasham, the Guildford printer, published the *Surrey Magazine* in the 1890s, he chose a young couple as a cover design to represent the county. One was

*A typical Surrey-type smock or 'round frock' of plain,
natural linen but finely stitched.*

a farm girl in an apron and sun-bonnet, the other a young wood-
cutter in a smock. This was pure nostalgia. By that date farm

The sandy soil round Elstead was relatively infertile, but well-suited for growing carrots, whose roots thrust deep into the thirsty soil. Here a group of carrot diggers pose, the man on the right with a special carrot trowel.

workers had become a small and shrinking minority, and the smock had vanished from the harvest field.

As the traditional Harvest Home disappeared, the church Harvest Festival was introduced. The awesomely-bad poet Martin Tupper of Albury wrote *A Hymn for the Harvest of 1847, composed for the thanksgiving day*, and by the early 1870s churches were being decorated with produce, and special hymns were sung. As J.H. Knight of Farnham observed, it was ironic that the church began officially to celebrate the farming year at exactly the time that local agriculture entered the long decline from which it never recovered.

Wheelwrights did not harvest, of course, but their equivalent of the Harvest Home was the 'waygoose', a supper party with songs to celebrate the completion of a new waggon.

In the south of the county it was common to find farms with cider-apple orchards, and we shall be encountering them again during the Christmas wassailing. Cider-making was carried out on a small scale, with hand-operated mills and presses. The apples were first crushed between the rollers of the cider mill and then the pulp folded into coarse fabric cloths. These were laid in a stack in a cider press, and then squeezed under the screw. The juice that ran out was then fermented in a vat, using the natural yeast on the apple skin. The resulting cider was put in casks, perhaps ready to refresh the workmen in the hay meadows and harvest fields the following year.

Hallowe'en was not associated with any particular customs in old Surrey. The traditions we observe today are a fairly recent introduction. The great night at this time of the year was Bonfire Night. The failure of Guy Fawkes' gunpowder plot on 5th November 1605 became a cause for national celebration, and Parliament ordered special church services to commemorate it each year. Churchwardens' accounts for many Surrey parishes record payments made to bellringers on the day of 'Gunpowder Treason'. In Pyrford this was done as late as 1817. By that time, however, 5th November had become more famous as Bonfire Night, with fires, fireworks and disorder.

Fires and fireworks may have soon become associated with the day. Certainly by 1739 Puttenham had a bonfire on the night of the 'Powder Plot', and by 1768 fireworks were being let off in the streets of Godalming. As with the Jack o' Lent, this was an opportunity for the local people to show their dislike of an unpopular local figure by making an effigy of him and then burning it on the bonfire. In 1830 it was the Bishop of Winchester himself who was hung in effigy at Farnham. However, William Stevens prevented the indignity of the Bishop's effigy being burnt by secretly carrying it away and burying it in his garden in Castle Street.

Harvests and Bonfires

The same tradition is described in Reigate in 1837. 'It has been the custom for many years to hang an effigy of some individual who may have made himself ridiculous or odious in the course of the year on the anniversary of St Crispin [25th October] and this taking place in the middle of the night accompanied by horrid yells and the firing of bombs, as they are called, alarms very much many of the timid females of the town ... The same figure being taken down in the morning is reserved to make a Guy Fawkes for the 5th November, when a monstrous fire is lighted in the Square... producing imminent danger of fire to the adjoining houses.' The magistrates attempted to put a stop to the disorders, and arrested some of the ringleaders. However, the mob, 'assisted as they were by an incursion of barbarians from the northern reaches about Walton Heath', almost succeeded in releasing them.

The gangs which organised the bonfires in early Victorian Surrey were usually known as the 'Guys' or the 'Bonfire Boys'. They would often be in disguise or fancy dress, perhaps to avoid recognition. The fires, built in the main streets of the towns, were assembled that night, the young men of the surrounding countryside bringing wood and other burnable material with them. Sometimes there would be a torchlight procession, headed by a band. As the guy was burnt on the fire, a rhyme was often chanted. The version used at Frensham ran:

> *Remember, remember the 5th of November,*
> *The Gunpowder Plot will never be forgot.*
> *Father and son shall tell of the day,*
> *And always remember old Guy Fawkes' Day.*

Old tar barrels, their ends knocked out and the interior set alight, were rolled blazing through the streets. The fireworks were home-made; gunpowder was easy to purchase and iron filings readily obtained from the blacksmith's forge to produce bright sparks. As in Reigate, the huge squibs or bangers could more accurately be called bombs. Huge jumping-jacks, known as

'serpents' (for they were the size and shape of the musical instrument of that name), could leap over a house roof at each explosion. The inhabitants of the town centre would shutter their windows and cover up their cellar gratings to keep the fireworks out. Those that had displeased the mob during the year may not just have had their effigy burnt. Their houses might be the target of the Guys' explosive attentions.

As with Shrove Tuesday football, Kingston was quick to put a stop to public disorder and the Market Square bonfire was suppressed in 1840 by the Metropolitan Police. However, in other parts of Surrey matters actually grew worse. The notorious Guy Riots in Guildford were stopped with military assistance in 1864, but Godalming, too, saw disturbances that night. A fire was built in the street at the junction with Mill Lane, and two special constables sworn in to maintain law and order were severely beaten up. For the next few years, the Surrey newspapers were full of court proceedings following Bonfire Night, as the police struggled to keep tar barrels and fireworks off the streets. In 1866, for example, there were prosecutions at Walton-on-Thames, Cobham and Esher. The Haslemere bonfire continued on Shepherd's Hill until the end of the custom in 1876. At Dorking the dangerous proceedings were ended, not by confrontation, but by strategy. Mr Heathfield Young provided beer and firewood at Cotmandene, safely away from the town centre.

The *Surrey Comet* was scathing in its report on the 5th of November celebrations at Richmond in 1874. 'Some of the elder juveniles – for they certainly do not deserve to be dignified with the appellation of men – had amused themselves ... by preparing effigies [of two local figures] and with these ... they sallied forth to inform the inhabitants of Richmond that "they knew no reason (as if their opinion were worth anything) why gunpowder treason should ever be forgot." ... if some persons were not foolish enough to give money to these skulkers who go about rattling coppers in boxes, under the plea of keeping up an old custom ...

HARVESTS AND BONFIRES

By the time this photograph of the Mint, Godalming was taken, the dangerous and disorderly scenes of bonfire night were only a memory.

the disgraceful scenes which sometimes take place would be witnessed no more.'

In fact, the anarchy of the traditional bonfire night was either stamped out altogether or tamed. This taming involved moving the fire to a safe place, and having a respectable committee organise the proceedings. Some traditional elements remained, however, as noted in Arthur Beadell's reminiscences of Warlingham in late Victorian times. 'On 5th November we had a first class bonfire on the old Recreation Ground. We boys collected a lot of bushes, waggon loads were brought by farmers and Mr Ward brought out waggon loads of shavings from his carpenters' shops. A guy was made and fixed to a pole at the top of the heap. Most of the boys wore masks which could be purchased in the village for the modest sum of a penny. Fireworks were also available in plenty. Men and boys paraded the village, duly made up in all sorts of dress and black faces by those who had no masks.'

Clement is the patron saint of blacksmiths, and it was customary for Surrey blacksmiths to 'fire the anvil' on St Clement's Day, 23rd November. This involved packing a small charge of gunpowder (no doubt left over from the 5th) into the tool-hole in the face of the anvil and touching it off with the tip of an iron rod made red-hot in the forge hearth. The explosion would be more impressive if a wooden plug was hammered down on top of the gunpowder.

The dark evenings around the cottage fire were suitable occasions for ghost stories. Belief in ghosts was universal, and is still widespread. People not infrequently report seeing mysterious figures, often in outdated clothing, which suddenly vanish. These may best be termed 'apparitions', and whether they belong to the realms of folklore or to some other aspect of the human experience is not for me to say. What I do claim for folklore, however, is the ghost story, the tale woven around the apparition to explain it. Probably hundreds of such stories have been told, enjoyed a brief moment of fame and then been forgotten. Few have been written down, and of those that have it is remarkable how even fewer are still current. When enquiring at a house or location said to have been haunted a hundred years ago, it is rare to find that the present occupants have noticed anything out of the ordinary. Let one stand for many.

An old house on the street in Bramley stands beside a stream that passes beneath the road. The apparition of a young girl in white was sometimes seen, standing where a door used to be, though later blocked up. The story is told that this tragic figure is the ghost of girl who threw herself into the water and drowned, following a broken love affair. She is no longer seen, and the tale might perhaps be considered a trifle unlikely. The stream is so shallow that drowning in it would be a difficult feat.

On some occasions, the visits of important figures seem to have made such an impact that their spirits were left behind them, at least in the minds of local people. Charles I spent a night at Vernon House in West Street, Farnham and was said to haunt the staircase there. The Duke of Monmouth was held prisoner in the iron-barred muniment room in the gate-tower of Abbot's Hospital on Guildford High Street for one night in 1685. His ghost, it is said, makes it impossible for any to spend the night there alone. In Godalming, the King's Arms Royal Hotel is said to be haunted by Tsar Peter the Great, who stayed there in 1698. He manifests his presence by the noise of a pair of heavy boots falling in the darkest hours of the night. None of these royal personages actually died in the places they are said to haunt, but their almost legendary status was evidently enough to confer a special atmosphere on them.

Perhaps one might almost have expected the ghost of Christopher Slaughterford to haunt Guildford High Street, for it was there he was hanged in 1709. He was accused of murdering his sweetheart and leaving her body in a sand pit near Losely. However, there was insufficient evidence to convict him and he was acquitted. Nevertheless, local people were convinced of his guilt and he stood a second trial. This time he was condemned, despite protesting his innocence. He was hanged on a gallows at Tunsgate: no doubt the mayor and corporation had a good view from the balcony of the Guildhall across the street. It was not long afterwards, though, that his apparition was seen 'in a sad and astonishing manner, in several dreadful and frightful shapes with a rope about his neck, a flaming torch in one hand and a

club in the other, crying "Vengeance! Vengeance!" '. Could it be that those who saw him were haunted by something more tangible: a feeling that they might, after all, have hanged an innocent man?

A painting hanging in the hall at Tadworth Court is the focus of another ghostly tale. It depicts a girl in a white dress, but behind her another girl's face appears mysteriously from among some leaves. The two were supposed to have been sisters in love with the same man, but it was the girl in the white dress who became engaged to him. One day, she leant over the landing rail to greet her lover as he arrived in the hall below. The other sister, struck by jealousy, rushed up behind and tipped her over the banister onto the stone floor of the hallway. She was killed instantly. The murderess then fled upstairs to the top floor, where she threw herself to her death. The legend relates that as long as the painting remains undisturbed, all will be well. However, if it is moved, then ghostly sounds will re-enact the tragedy.

Needless to say, there is no historical foundation on which to base this story. The painting is probably of the late 17th century and the parish registers of Banstead have no record of two sisters of marriageable age dying on the same day in that period. Furthermore, the style of the dress is Dutch or Flemish, not English, and the ghostly face among the foliage belongs to an earlier picture which was painted over. One imagines the tale was created to explain the picture, rather than the other way round.

There have always been those ready to take advantage of other people's superstitious fears, however. One such incident occurred at an inn in Godalming High Street in 1867. A group of local tradesmen were drinking in the snug late one evening when they were interrupted. The barmaid rushed in, clearly distressed and claiming to have seen a ghost. She had been in the back garden of the inn when she encountered a white-shrouded figure with horns and glittering eyes. The drinkers, after some discussion, decided to go out together to see what they could find. There was no ghost to be seen, though they did bump into each other in the dark and so frightened themselves. However, a local greengrocer crept round to the rear of the garden by a different route, and came across a white figure hurrying the other way. When he grabbed it, a series of shrill screams came forth. Dragging the figure back into the warmth and light of the inn, the horns, sheet and other parts of the disguise were pulled off in the presence of the valiant ghost hunters. Underneath was one of the chambermaids of the inn, who had thought to have a joke at the barmaid's expense.

Personally, I have never seen a ghost and my attitude is that of a countryman who, when asked if he believed in ghosts, replied, 'Oh no, but I'm mortal afeared of them.'

Towards the end of November comes the Twenty-fifth Sunday after Trinity, or Stir Up Sunday, as it was known. The collect for the day began 'Stir up, we beseech thee, O Lord, the wills of thy faithful people', which the country folk took as a sign that they were to mix the ingredients for their plum puddings, for Christmas was drawing near.

CHAPTER 6

The Christmas Season

Advent Sunday falls around the beginning of December, signalling a time of fasting and preparation for the great festival of Christmas. It would be hard to think of any greater contrast between the way the weeks before Christmas were spent then and the way they are now. In old Surrey, it was the twelve days following Christmas that were the time of merry-making and indulgence, not the twelve – or more – days before it.

The days were still growing shorter and colder. The shortest day of the year is 21st December, St Thomas' Day, as noted in the rhyme:

St Thomas gray, St Thomas gray,
The longest night and the shortest day.

In Surrey, it was the day the old folk went 'gooding'. 'It was the custom in Puttenham on St Thomas Day as in most other places for the old people to go 'a-gooding', when they visited the houses of the wealthier class for the dole which was usually provided for them. Mr Daniel Simmonds of Rodsall distributed to each a gain [a gallon?] of rye, which was ground for them by Mrs Valler of

THE CHRISTMAS SEASON

The farmers around Chertsey were noted for their generosity towards the gooders on St Thomas' Day in early Victorian times. However, times were to change.

Cutt Mill. Some of them made pancakes of the meal, and otherwise employed it in their Christmas festivities. John Winter remembers the old women of Puttenham (many of them with red cloaks over their bonnets), trotting about on St Thomas' Day, bent on collecting their 'goodings'.'

At Chaldon, a gallon of wheat was usual, with the farmer's wife giving perhaps some clothing or cake. At Chertsey, it was the intention to collect the ingredients for a Christmas pudding. Recalling the 1850s, an old lady said, 'I remember it as if it were yesterday ... We used to go out with our sacks and our bags ... Some folks 'ud say, "Well and what do you want?" when we knocked at the door, pretending as they didn't know; and then we made our curtseys and says, "Please remember the Gooders, Ma'am!" And some 'ud give money, and some flour, or currants and raisins, and shovel 'em into our bags: there was farmer Johnson, as mother worked for, he always ground two sacks o' corn for the Gooders; and he used to stand at his door ... and give it out ... Ah, farmers was different i' them days.'

The link between St Thomas' Day and generosity to the poor made it a popular time for charities to be distributed. Bread was

C. Childerstone, a poulterer on Guildford High Street, shows off his Christmas display in about 1870. Turkeys have already overtaken geese as the favourite fowl.

given out at Thames Ditton, Godstone and Farnham, while at Worplesdon beer, and at Charlwood beef, were also provided. In Kingston, Norton's Charity was originally intended to provide wood for the poor to warm them through the winter, but by Victoria's reign a shilling was being given to 20 widows instead.

As Christmas drew near, the shopkeepers in the towns put on special displays of their wares. The butcher arranged his finest beef, sometimes adorned with rosettes awarded to the animals at fatstock shows. The grocers would exhibit dried fruit and all the ingredients of plum puddings, decorated with holly. It was the poulterer, though, whose display was most extravagant. Geese and turkeys were becoming more popular by mid-Victorian times as alternatives to the traditional beef for Christmas dinner, and they were joined by ducks, pheasants and other game.

The wine merchant did not lag behind, either. But wines and spirits were for the wealthier classes. The villagers' tipple at Christmas time was home-made elderberry wine, warmed up so that the aromatic flavour was brought out. Friends and neighbours who called to wish the compliments of the season would be sure to be offered a glass. A cheesemonger in Kingston named Pamphilon would always have hot elder wine for his customers when they came in with their Christmas orders.

In the days before Christmas bands, waits and carol-singers would come round performing the traditional music of the season. It is sad to reflect how limited our modern repertoire of carols has become. Now, there are perhaps only a couple of dozen carols sung; sung not only throughout England, but the English-speaking world. In the earlier 19th century there were hundreds, each district priding itself on its local carols. Crowhurst, Lingfield and Dormansland had different tunes for the same words, for example. Many, perhaps most, of these local versions have been lost. Some, however, have been written down, like 'Here comes Poor Jack', sung by groups of Surrey boys collecting money.

Here comes poor Jack a-howling,
And don't know what to say!
Please give him a few ha'pence
And let him run away!
A pocket full of money,
A cellar full of beer!
I wish you a merry Christmas
And a happy New Year!

'The Moon Shines Bright' was published by the Rev. Broadwood of Newdigate in 1843, as one of the songs sung at his house by visiting carol singers:

In St Mary's, Oxted the backs of the pews were drilled
to take sprigs of evergreen at Christmas.

THE CHRISTMAS SEASON

The moon shines bright, and the stars give a light,
In a little time it will be day;
The Lord our God he calls upon us all,
And bids us awake and pray.
Awake, awake, good people all,
Awake and you shall hear
How Christ was born all upon this morn
For the Lord loved us so dear.

The carol then calls on all to repent and concludes,

Now my song is done, and I must be gone,
No longer can I tarry here;
So God bless you all, both great and small,
And send you a happy new year.

'The Moon Shines Bright' is one of the old carols which used to be sung only on Christmas Night, that is the time between midnight and dawn on 25th December. At Dorking the town band roused the inhabitants with the tune 'Get up! Get up! and put the pudding in the pot'. The church bells would ring out for the Christmas service. Usually the churchgoers would find the church itself decorated for the season. The backs of the pews of Oxted church were drilled with small holes to take sprigs of holly, for example; a practice that was common elsewhere. The pulpit, reading desk and candelabra of Dorking church were similarly decked in greenery.

Homes, too, had their Christmas decorations. As an account from Reigate in 1827 relates, 'Then may be seen the windows, the mantel-pieces, and the well-arranged kitchen shelves, clothed with the green holly with its scarlet berry, while in the hall of the hospitable mansion, in the farm house, and even in the humble labourer's cottage, the mystic mistletoe has its share of attraction – frequently being suspended from the ceiling, in a large cluster of boughs rich in green leaves and white berries – the mirth-exciting

*St Peter and St Paul, Lingfield decorated with greenery at
Christmas time in the Edwardian period.*

challenger of youth, and the test of maiden coyness. Every kiss
beneath it is entitled to the forfeiture of a berry fresh plucked from
the bough; and it sometimes happens that ere the Christmas
holidays are over the branches and the leaves are all that can be
seen of the mistletoe!'

The Christmas tree, made popular by the young Queen
Victoria's court in the 1840s, began to replace the kissing-bough
as the centrepiece of the decorations. William Wade, a Guildford
confectioner, was selling sweets to decorate Christmas trees by
1851.

Christmas dinner was eaten soon after returning from church.
While today 'dinner' has generally come to mean an evening meal,

many of us still dine at noon or one o'clock on Christmas Day in the old way. The roast beef – or poultry – was washed down with strong beer or elder wine, and followed by plum pudding. Grace was generally said at the end of the meal, not the beginning. The simple Surrey grace was, 'Thank God for my good belly full!'

For the twelve days following Christmas, farm work was kept to a minimum. We must not forget the dairy farmer, however, who never has respite from the demands of his cows. The cows and the other farm animals also partook of the Christmas cheer, being given the best corn and the best hay. This was a time when parties were held and games were played, such as Snap Dragon, in which sultanas had to be picked out of a bowl of burning brandy. Fiddles would be played for dancing, and sometimes the old-fashioned pipe and tabor as well. A pipe and tabor player named Hilton entertained the households of the Dorking area in the early 19th century, the little drum keeping time to the tune of his three-finger pipe. Employers would also have parties for their workmen. The widow of William Keen, a Farnham wheelwright, recalled how she and her husband would invite the workmen into their best room for hot elderberry wine. Even the rough-and-ready sawyers were included: 'I think people used to be happier then. They weren't so stuck up. There wasn't so much difference between the classes, but t'was more like a family.'

Boxing Day saw the tradesmen who had come to the house during the previous year come once more with solicitous wishes for a happy New Year. They expected, and usually received, a small sum in return.

The weather was carefully noted, as we have come to expect. *A dark Christmas makes a heavy wheatsheaf* meant that if no moon shone at Christmas then a good harvest would follow in the coming year. *A green Yule makes a full churchyard* observed that a Christmas without frost or snow would be unhealthy.

*This group in fancy dress is actually collecting for the Royal Surrey
County Hospital at Shamley Green in 1898. However, some
of the costumes are similar to those worn by the tipteerers.
(Shamley Green Local History Society)*

The Christmas season was the time that the tipteerers put in
their appearance. At least, they were known as 'tipteerers' in the
south of the county: in the north 'mummers' was more usual.
They were a group of strangely-costumed players who toured the
villages and farmsteads, acting out a short drama. Essentially, the
play was always the same, although details varied from place to
place. One by one, the characters step forward and announce who
they are. Two then fight with wooden swords and one is killed. A
doctor is summoned, who brings the dead man back to life. Other

The Christmas Season

Lady Bray of Shere Manor, at the time this photograph was taken, gave Christmas gifts of blankets and material to local widows.

characters then enter and the play ends with an appeal for money. The characters speak in doggerel rhymes, which were handed down by word of mouth and so became garbled over the years. The villainous Turkish Knight is often corrupted to 'Turkey Snipe', for example.

The characters usually included Father Christmas, King George, Turkey Snipe, and the Doctor. Amongst the others could be Billy Whittle, the Valiant Soldier, Beelzebub and Little Johnny Jack, 'with my wife and family on my back' (he had dolls hung down the back of his costume). In earlier times, the tipteerers wore

clothes covered in strips of paper or rags, which they also hung down from the brims of hats or other headgear as a disguise. Later a more 'amateur dramatic' spirit seems to have entered into the costumes, with attempts to dress the part: King George with a crown, the Valiant Soldier in uniform, and so on.

The tipteerers, numbering between six and nine, met before Christmas to go through their parts. At Frensham in the 1870s they would camp at Hammond's Wood and the clashing of their wooden swords as they rehearsed the fight could be heard half a mile away. Then the evening tours would begin, performing in the hallways of the grand houses and the cosy kitchens of the farms. The village pub was certain to be visited. Often the tipteerers also sang carols: 'The Twelve Joys of Mary' and 'God rest ye merry, gentlemen' were especially popular. The money collected after the performance would be divided among the players. At Thames Ditton the method of distributing the contents of the heavy money bag was simple: 'As none would feel in the mood for any exact mathematics, the money would be tipped on to a table and divided up with the faithful sword into the required number of heaps, one for each though by this method their value would differ much!'

It must not be imagined that the standard of acting was very high. The mummers came to George Sturt's cottage in Lower Bourne on the night of 27th December 1897. Afterwards he wrote, 'I have to admit that as play-acting it was incomparably the very worst thing I have ever seen.' A.J. Munby of Wheeler's Farm, Pyrford had another visit on the evening of New Year's Day 1883: 'A party of mummers performed outside my house – half a dozen grown men, all wearing grotesque masks, strange hats, smocks or other guise over their clothes, all singing 'God rest ye merry gentlemen', most mournfully, to the music of an old accordion. I did not comprehend these vagrom men, but gave them a coin, as who should say, "We may never see the likes of you again." '

Munby was a little premature in predicting the end of the tipteerers. They were a common part of the Surrey Christmas for another 30 years, until the First World War largely put an end to that tradition, as to so much else. Nevertheless, the mummers continued to tour Esher, Claygate and the Dittons until the 1930s.

The New Year was marked at midnight by the church bells ringing the old year out and the new in. New Year's Day was the time to exchange gifts, rather than the modern custom of presents on the morning of Christmas Day. The poor were not forgotten by the gentry. Around Christmas at the end of Victoria's reign, Lady Bray of Shere Manor gave dress materials and blankets to local widows, while the Gilliats of Levylsdene, Merrow gave a hundredweight of coal and a box of groceries to those who had attended church regularly.

Wassailing – from the old Saxon toast *'wæs hæl'*, 'be healthy' – was a distinctive Christmas custom. This was another door-to-door visiting, with the expectation of food, drink, and a little money. The wassailers in return would wish the household good luck for the coming year. The wassail bowl was sometimes carried, a wooden bowl to be filled with spiced ale or cider and passed round the company for each to take a drink. The Rev. Broadwood wrote down one of the wassailing songs at Newdigate in the opening years of Victoria's reign:

A wassail, a wassail, a wassail we begin,
With sugar plums and cinnamon, and other spices in;
With a wassail, a wassail, a jolly wassail,
And may joy come to you, and to our wassail.

Good Master and good mistress, as you sit by the fire,
Consider us poor wassailers, who travel through the mire,
With a wassail, a wassail, a jolly wassail,
And may joy come to you, and to our wassail.

*Good master and good mistress, if you will be but
willing,*
*Come send us out your eldest son with a sixpence or a
shilling*
  With a wassail, a wassail, a jolly wassail,
  And may joy come to you, and to our wassail.
*Good master and good mistress, if thus it should you
please,*
*Come send us out your white loaf, likewise your
Christmas cheese,*
  With a wassail, a wassail, a jolly wassail,
  And may joy come to you, and to our wassail.

*The Six Bells, Newdigate. Singers on the Surrey-Sussex border
had a vigorous tradition of local carols and wassailing
songs at Christmas.*

The Christmas Season

In the southern, cider-drinking parishes of the county, the wassailers sometimes would 'wassail' the cider-apple trees as well. This involved the party surrounding a representative tree in the orchard, and the following rhyme (or variants of it) would be recited:

Here stands a good old apple-tree!
Stand fast at root,
Bear well at top;
Every little twig
Bear an apple big:
Every little bough
Bear an apple now.
Hots full! rapfifull!
Threescore sacksfull!
Hullo, boys, hullo!

Then a long, loud shouting began, the trunk of the tree was rapped with sticks and finally a cow's horn was blown. The company would then retire to the farmhouse for elder wine and other refreshments.

Twelfth Night, on 6th January, was the Feast of the Epiphany and last day of the Christmas holiday. The centrepiece of the entertainment that evening was the Twelfth Cake. This could be home-made, or bought from confectioners in the towns. Richly-iced and decorated fruit cakes, they contained little rolled up scraps of paper with the names of characters on them, and often verses as well. One character was always the king, another the queen, and whoever found them in their slice of cake must take on that role for the evening, until midnight struck and Christmas was over for another year.

An ancient song from Elstead records the Twelfth Night revels:

Now farewell good Christmas, adieu and adieu,
Quickly I leave thee and look for a new.
Until thou returnest I linger in pain,
And I care not how quickly thou comest again.

But ere thou departest I purpose to see
What merry good pastime this day will give me;
For a king of our wassail this night we must choose,
Or else the old custom we carelessly lose.

Shalford Street decorated for an agricultural show in 1871.

The wassail well spiced about shall go round
Though it cost my good master best part of a pound.
The maid in the buttery stands ready to fill
Her nappy [strong] good liquor with heart and good will.

To welcome us kindly our master stands by,
And tells me in friendship one tooth is a-dry.
Now we will accept it like lovingly friends,
And so for this Christmas my carol here ends.

At Hascombe as elsewhere, it was believed that Christmas greenery should be burnt, not thrown away, or otherwise bad luck

Shamley Green, a typical Surrey village, in a photograph taken
at a time when the old way of life was rapidly being
replaced by the new.

would follow. There are still many today who hold to this superstition, and it is typical of those which can survive within a family long after the communal customs of the village have been swept away by incomers.

So, with the end of Christmas, the eternal circle of the farming year begins again, its passage through time marked by milestones of custom and tradition. One by one, however, these milestones have crumbled or been removed. It has been said that the mother of folklore is poverty, but poverty is not the same as ignorance. One educationalist wrote of Surrey in 1844 that 'the intellect of the working class has long been suffered to lie as dead and as barren as one of their own sand-hills'. This patronising attitude was common but misplaced. The people knew well what they needed to know to earn their living from the soil. They knew the beauty of a love song, the enjoyment of a dance, the thrill of a scary or mysterious story. Above all, they knew this was their own culture, not that of the gentry or the incomer.

It was not to last. Education was seen as the way out of poverty and if this robbed the villager of his own local culture, then it was a price worth paying. George Sturt, in *Change in the Village* depicts the intense poverty of mid-Victorian life in his beloved Bourne, just outside Farnham. He also makes painfully clear the sense of loss felt by himself and others as the old way of life faded into memory. Land prices rose as gentlemanly dwellings were built to house newcomers, none of whom earned their living in the village itself. The old ways ended, and with them the undoubted suffering and privation which was taken for granted. With them passed also the culture of the people. Nevertheless, enough has been preserved to show that our county had as rich and varied a folklore as any in the land.

INDEX

Abinger   62, 63
Albury   63
Alfold   20, *21*
April Fool's Day   38
Ascension Day   63
Ash Wednesday   27
Aubrey, John   14

Banstead   *19*, 108
Beddington   59
Bonfire Night   102–106
Bramley   63, 104
Broadwater   95
Brockham Green   61
broomsquires   *85*, 86

Candlemas   15, 28
Carshalton   40, *59*, 78
Chaldon   111
Chertsey   57, *111*
child labour   56–57, 70, 72
children's games   72
Chobham   *39*, 40, 56
cider-making   102
Cobham   45, 104
cock-shying   20
Compton   *9*, 16, 59
Crack Nut Sunday   80–81
Croydon   40, 56, 57

Devil's Jumps   65–66, *67*
Devil's Punchbowl (Highcomb
   Bottom)   65, *85*, 89
Dorking   *15*, 23, 24–27, *26*, 27, 38,
   57, 63, 64, 68, 75, 104, 115, 117
Dunsfold   50, 53

Easter   17, 49–52

Elstead   17, *101*
Epsom   40, *41*
Ewell   40, *41*, 50
Ewhurst   27, 29

fairies: see 'pharisees'
fairs   44, 68, 76, 81, *84*, 86, 94
Farncombe   *71*
Farnham   *57*, *58*, 64, 69, 91, 92, 94,
   95, 102, 107, 113
feuds and fights   67–68
firing the anvil   106
folk remedies   78
Forest Green   63
Frensham   43, 64–66, 103, 120

Garland Day   *59*, 60, *61*, 62
ghosts   106–109
Godalming   27, *42*, 51, 102, 104,
   105, 107, 108
Good Friday   45–49
gooding   110
Grotter Day   77
grottoes   76–77
Guildford   10, 30, 40, 42, 45, 46,
   56, 57, 63, 68, 69,83–86, 104,
   107, *112*
Guildford Guys   85, 104

Hambledon   27, 60
harvest home   95–98
Hascombe   43, *70*, 125
Haslemere   50, 51, *52*, 104
Hindhead   86, *88*, 89
hop picking   91–92, *93*
husband-divining   14, 16

Jack in the Green   57

INDEX

Jack o' Lent, riding the   51–53

Kerry, Rev. Francis   59, 74, 80
Kingston-upon-Thames   21, *22*,
    24, *56*, 57, 58, 80, *82*, 104,
    113

lavender growing   77
Leatherhead   81
Limpsfield   45

May Day   44, 55–63
May garlands   59–60, *61*, 62, 63
maypole dancing   62
maypoles   *55–56*
Merrow school   62
Michaelmas   81, 83
Mitcham   40, 57, 76–78
Molesey   56
Mortlake   *18*, 19
morris dancing   57–59
Mothering Sunday   28
Mother Ludlam   65, 66

Newdigate   63, 114, *122*
New Year's Day   121

Oak Apple Day   64
Ockley   59, 75
Oxted   *114*, 115

Palm Sunday   43, 44
pancake bell   19
Petersham   56
'pharisees' (fairies)   79–80
Pirbright   38, 39–40
Pudding Pie Sunday: see Mothering
    Sunday
Puttenham   50, 59, 74, 102, 110
Pyrford   102, 120

Reigate   69, 103, 115
Richmond   104
Ruskin, John   62

Seale   98
Sherborne   44
Shik Shak Day: see Oak Apple Day
Shrove Tuesday (Pancake Day)
    18–22
shroving   20
smocks   *31*, 98–99, *100*, 101
'Snap Dragon'   117
St Agnes' Eve   14
St Catherine's Hill, near Guildford
    83, *84*
St Clement's Day   106
Stir-up Sunday   109
St John's Eve   74
St Martha's Hill, near Guildford   *46*,
    47, 83
street football   21–27
St Swithin's Day   75
St Thomas' Day   111
Sturt, George   19, *37* (capt.), 57, 63,
    120, 126
St Valentine's Day   16
Surrey speech   33, 43
Surrey Union hunt   33, *34*

Thames Ditton   113, 120
Thursley   86, *87*, 89
twelfth cake   123
Twelfth Night   123–124
tipteerers   *118*, 119–121
Titsey   50
tithes   92
'Tingling'   44

wassailing   121, *122*, 123
waygoose   101
weather predictions   16, 36–38, 51,
    75, 117
Whitelands Training College   62
Whitsun   64
Witley   64, *65*
Wonersh   98, *99*
Worplesdon   56, 113
yew   43–44